Adoption Now

ADOPTION AND CHILDREN ACT 2002 LAW, REGULATIONS, GUIDANCE AND STANDARDS (ENGLAND)

Roy Stewart with
Alexandra Conroy Harris

CoramBAAF Adoption and Fostering Academy
41 Brunswick Square
London WC1N 1AZ
www.corambaaf.org.uk

Coram Academy Limited, registered as a company limited by guarantee in England and Wales number 9697712, part of the Coram group, charity number 312278

© Roy Stewart with Alexandra Conroy Harris, 2024
Previous editions: 2006, 2011, 2013, BAAF

British Library Cataloguing in Publication Data
A catalogue record for this book is available from the British Library

ISBN 978 1 913384 33 3

Designed and typeset by Helen Joubert Design
Printed in the UK by The Lavenham Press

All rights reserved. Except as permitted under the Copyright, Designs and Patents Act 1988, this publication may not be reproduced, stored in a retrieval system, or transmitted in any form or by any means, without the prior written permission of the publisher.

No part of this publication may be reproduced without the written consent of the author.

Contents

Part I Principles, concepts & statutory provisions	**3**
Introduction	4
Principles and concepts	5
The adoption service	8
Authorisation to place and consequences of placement	15
Consequences of placement	22
Removal of children who are or may be placed by adoption agencies	28
Removal of children in non-agency case	32
Adoption orders	36
Disclosure of information	45
Status of adopted children	50
The Registers	52
Adoptions with a foreign element	55
Miscellaneous	60
Special guardianship	66
Advertisements and Adoption and Children Act Register	75
Part II Regulations	**79**
Fostering for Adoption	80
Regulations	81
The Adoption Agencies Regulations 2005	81
The Adoption Support Services Regulations 2005	105
The Independent Review of Determinations (Adoption & Fostering) Regulations 2009	115
The Adoptions with a Foreign Element Regulations 2005	117
The Adopted Children and Adoption Contact Registers Regulations 2005	127
The Adoption Information and Intermediary Services (Pre-Commencement Adoptions) Regulations 2005	129
The Disclosure of Adoption Information (Post-Commencement Adoptions) Regulations 2005	133

The Restriction on the Preparation of Adoption Reports Regulations 2005	137
The Suitability of Adopters Regulations 2005	138
Adoption Support Agencies (England) and Adoption Agencies (Miscellaneous Amendments) Regulations 2005	140
The Special Guardianship Regulations 2005	144

Part III National Minimum Standards	**153**
National Minimum Standards Adoption Agencies	154
Child & service user focused standards	155
Adoption agency and adoption support agency standards	186
Appendix 1: Source material	**217**
Index	**219**

Abbreviations
All references in brackets are to the Adoption and Children Act 2002 (ACA 2002) unless otherwise stated.

CA 1989 = Children Act 1989
C&YPA 2008 = Children and Young Persons Act 2008
C&FA 2014 = Children and Families Act 2014
E&AA 2016 = Education and Adoption Act 2016

Notes about the authors

Roy Stewart is an independent child care consultant and trainer, an independent chair of adoption and fostering panels and Director of RIKS Consultancy Ltd. Roy has extensive experience as a practitioner and manager in local authority and voluntary sector adoption and fostering services. He is the co-author of *Adoption Now (Adoption Act 1976)* (BAAF, 2003), *Adoption Now (Adoption and Children Act 2002)* (BAAF, 2006, 2011 and 2013 editions), and *Adoption & Children (Scotland) Act 2007 – The Act & Regulations* (BAAF, 2011).

Alexandra Conroy Harris is CoramBAAF's Legal Consultant. She is a barrister with over twenty years' experience of representing parents, children and local authorities in care and adoption proceedings. She spent nine years as a senior social services lawyer for a London borough, during which she was a committed user of this guide's previous edition. She has worked for BAAF/CoramBAAF since 2008 and produces the Legal Notes for the *Adoption & Fostering* journal.

Acknowledgements

Thanks are due to Fergus Smith, now retired, who co-authored the original and subsequent revised editions of *Adoption Now*.

Note to this edition

This edition has been updated to reflect significant changes introduced by the Children and Families Act 2014 and the Children and Social Work Act 2017, provision for Regional Adoption Agencies (RAAs) introduced by the Education and Adoption Act 2016, and revised National Minimum Standards issued in July 2014.

Note that proposed new statutory guidance issued for consultation in 2014 remains in draft form and has not been included in this edition.

PART I
PRINCIPLES, CONCEPTS
& STATUTORY PROVISIONS

Introduction

This updated guide is for use by those in England, whose work with children and their families involves or might involve adoption.

It is intended to provide easy access to and reinforce understanding of the Adoption and Children Act 2002 and its associated regulations, guidance and National Minimum Standards.

Part I of the book summarises the underpinning principles and concepts, as well as the main provisions of, the law.

It is laid out in the following order that reflects the anticipated needs of practitioners, and includes, where required, a brief reference to the relevant regulation:

- principles and concepts
- adoption service
- placement framework
- consequences of placement
- adoption orders
- disclosure of information
- status of adopted children
- the registers
- adoptions with a foreign element
- miscellaneous provisions
- special guardianship
- adverts and the Adoption and Children Act register

Part II offers a comprehensive summary of relevant regulations and cross references to relevant aspects of statutory guidance.

Part III provides a summary of the 2014 National Minimum Standards for adoption.

A subject index enables rapid access to specific subjects.

This guide should be used only to supplement, not replace, reference to source material and competent legal advice.

Principles and concepts

The ACA 2002 is founded upon the following overarching principles:

- **Paramountcy of the child's welfare throughout their life** – in all decisions by courts and adoption agencies, including whether to dispense with a parent's consent to adoption
- **A 'welfare checklist'** comparable to its Children Act 1989 equivalent but reflecting adoption-related issues
- **Avoidance of undue delay** in planning for permanence and adoption when children cannot be cared for by their birth family
- **No order** – unless the court considers that making the order would be better for the child than not doing so

The Act is also conceptually underpinned by its:

- enhancement of permanence options through extension (when appropriate) of child arrangements orders to 18 years and by introducing special guardianship;
- introduction of the possibility of unmarried couples adopting jointly;
- encouragement of people to adopt by obliging local authorities to ensure that support and required financial assistance are available to those affected by adoption;
- acknowledgement of the lifelong impact of adoption on all parties;

- establishment of a more consistent approach to the release of sensitive and identifying information contained in adoption records; and
- allowing birth families access to intermediary services.

Exercise of powers by court or adoption agency [s.1]

Section 1 applies whenever a court or adoption agency is coming to a decision relating to the adoption of a child [s.1(1)].

Chapter 8 of the Guidance gives detailed advice on agency duties in court proceedings including references to the Family Procedure Rules. It requires Directors of Children's Services to develop and sustain links with local courts to help minimise delays.

The paramount consideration of the court or adoption agency must be the child's welfare, throughout their life [s.1(2)].

The court or adoption agency must at all times bear in mind that, in general, any delay in coming to the decision is likely to prejudice the child's welfare [s.1(3)].

The court or adoption agency must have regard to the following matters (among others):

- the child's ascertainable wishes and feelings regarding the decision (considered in the light of their age and understanding);
- the child's particular needs;
- the likely effect on the child (throughout life) of having ceased to be a member of the original family and becoming an adopted person;
- the child's age, sex, background and any of the child's characteristics which the court or agency considers relevant;
- any harm (within the meaning of section 31(9) Children Act 1989 as amended) which the child has suffered or is at risk of suffering; and
- the relationship which the child has with relatives, with any prospective adopter with whom the child is placed, and with any

other person in relation to whom the court or agency considers it relevant, including the likelihood of any such relationship continuing and the value to the child of it doing so; the ability and willingness of any of the child's relatives, or of any such person, to provide the child with a secure environment in which the child can develop, and otherwise to meet the child's needs; and thirdly, the wishes and feelings of any of the child's relatives, or of any such person, regarding the child [s.1(4)].

Note: the original s.1(5) relating to the child's race, religion and culture was removed from English law by C&FA 2014 and now only applies in Wales.

The court or adoption agency must always consider the whole range of powers available to it in the child's case (whether under this Act or the Children Act 1989) and must not make any order under this Act unless it considers that making the order would be better for the child than not doing so [s.1(6)].

In section 1, 'coming to a decision relating to the adoption of a child', in relation to a court, includes:

- in any proceedings where the orders that might be made include the making or revoking of an adoption or placement order or making, varying or revoking a section 26 contact order, and

- making a decision about granting leave in respect of any action (other than initiation of proceedings in any court) which may be taken by an adoption agency or individual under this Act.

It does **not** include coming to a decision about granting leave in any other circumstances [s.1(7)].

For the purposes of section 1, references to relationships are not confined to legal relationships and references to a relative, in relation to a child, include the child's mother and father [s.1(8)].

The adoption service

Basic definitions [s.2]

The services maintained by local authorities under section 3(1) described below may be collectively referred to as 'the adoption service', and a local authority or registered adoption society may be referred to as an 'adoption agency' [s.2(1)].

A 'registered adoption society' means a voluntary organisation which is an adoption society registered under Part 2 of the Care Standards Act 2000.

In relation to the provision of any facility of the adoption service, references to a registered adoption society or an adoption agency do not include an adoption society which is not registered in respect of that facility [s.2(2)], i.e. under section 13(3) Care Standards Act 2000 the registration authority may attach a condition to registration including a condition that the body is not registered in respect of a particular facility.

A registered adoption society is to be treated as registered in respect of any facility of the adoption service unless it is a condition of its registration that it does not provide that facility [s.2(3)].

Adoption societies applying under Part 2 of the Care Standards Act 2000 must be incorporated bodies [s.2(4)].

In the ACA 2002:

- 'the 1989 Act' means the Children Act 1989;
- 'adoption society' means a body whose functions consist of or include making arrangements for the adoption of children;
- 'voluntary organisation' means a body other than a public or local authority the activities of which are not carried on for profit [s.2(5)]; and

- 'adoption support services' means counselling, advice and information, and any other services prescribed in the Adoption Support Services Regulations 2005 [s.2(6)].

The power to make regulations as referred to above, is to be exercised so as to secure that local authorities provide financial support [s.2(7)].

In sections 2–17 ACA 2002, references to adoption are to the adoption of persons, wherever they may be habitually resident, effected under the law of any country or territory, within or outside the British Islands [s.2(8)].

Maintenance of adoption service [s.3]

Each local authority must continue to maintain within its area (and for that purpose must provide the requisite facilities) a service designed to meet the needs, in relation to adoption, of:

- children who may be adopted, their parents and guardians;
- persons wishing to adopt a child; and
- adopted persons, their parents, natural parents and former guardians [s.3(1)].

Those facilities must include making, and participating in, arrangements for the:

- adoption of children; and
- provision of adoption support services [s.3(2)].

As part of the service, the arrangements made for the purposes of adoption support services:

- must extend to the provision of adoption support services to those described in the Adoption Support Services Regulations 2005; and
- may extend to the provision of those services to others [s.3(3)].

A local authority may provide any of the requisite facilities by securing its provision by:

The adoption service

- registered adoption societies; or
- others identified in regulation 5 of the Adoption Support Services Regulations 2005 of persons who may provide the facilities in question [s.3(4)].

The facilities must be provided in conjunction with the local authority's other social services and with registered adoption societies in its area, so that help may be given in a co-ordinated manner without duplication, omission or avoidable delay [s.3(5)].

The social services referred to in s.3(5) are the functions of a local authority which are social services functions within the meaning of the Local Authority Social Services Act 1970 [s.3(6)].

Regional adoption agencies

Amendments made by the Education and Adoption Act 2016 provide for the Secretary of State to direct local authorities to arrange for any or all of its functions to be carried out by another agency or agencies acting together [s.3ZA(1) & (2)].

The functions which may be so delegated are:

- *the recruitment, assessment and approval of prospective adopters;*
- *decisions as to whether a particular child should be placed with a particular prospective adopter (i.e. matching); and*
- *the provision of adoption support services [s.3ZA(3)].*

Assessments etc for adoption support services [s.4]

A local authority must carry out an assessment of that person's needs for adoption support services at the request of any:

- of the persons mentioned in s.3(1); or
- other person identified in regulation 13 of the Adoption Support Services Regulations 2005 [s.4(1)].

The adoption service

A local authority may, at the request of any person, carry out an assessment of that person's needs for adoption support services [s.4(2)].

A local authority *may* request the help of registered adoption societies or of persons identified in regulation 14 Adoption Support Services Regulations 2005 in carrying out an assessment [s.4(3)].

Where, as a result of an assessment, a local authority decides that a person has needs for adoption support services, it must then decide whether to provide any such services to that person [s.4(4)].

If the local authority decides to provide any adoption support services to a person, and the circumstances are as described in regulation 16 of the Adoption Support Services Regulations 2005:

- it must prepare a plan for their provision and keep the plan under review [s.4(5)].

Regulations made under section 4(6) make provision about assessments, preparing and reviewing plans, the provision of adoption support services in accordance with plans and reviewing the provision of adoption support services.

A local authority may carry out an assessment of the needs of any person under section 4 at the same time as an assessment of their needs is made under any other enactment [s.4(8)].

The local authority must notify the relevant health or education authority if at any time during the assessment of the needs of any person under section 4, it appears to it that there may be a need for the provision to that person of services from such authorities [s.4(9)].

Where it appears to a local authority that another local authority could, by taking any specified action, help in the exercise of any of its functions under section 4, it may request the help of that other authority, specifying the action in question [s.4(10)].

A local authority whose help is so requested must comply with the request if it is consistent with the exercise of its functions [s.4(11)].

Local authority plans for adoption services [s.5]

Section 64 Children Act 2004 repealed the obligation introduced by section 5 ACA 2002 for production of local authority plans for adoption services and replaced it with an obligation under section 17 of that Act to produce regular 'children and young people's plans'.

De-registered, inactive or defunct adoption societies [ss.6&7]

There is a power for the appropriate Minister to direct such a society or, if necessary, the local authority to take appropriate action for the transfer of the functions of such a society.

Adoption support agencies [s.8]

In the ACA 2002, 'adoption support agency' means an 'undertaking' the purpose of which, or one of the purposes of which, is the provision of adoption support services; but an undertaking is not an adoption support agency:

- merely because it provides information in connection with adoption other than for the purpose mentioned in section 98(1) (assisting adopted adults to obtain information in relation to their adoption and facilitating contact between adopted adults and their birth families); or

- if it is excepted by virtue of section 8(2) summarised below [s.8(1)].

The following are for the purposes for section 8(1) 'excepted':

- a registered adoption society, whether or not registered in respect of provision of adoption support services;

- a local authority;

- a local education authority (within the meaning of the Education Act 1996);

- a Special Health Authority, Primary Care Trust (in Wales, a Health Authority or Local Health Board) or NHS trust;

- the Registrar General; or

The adoption service

- any person, or description of persons, excepted in regulation 4 of the Adoption Support Agencies (England) and Adoption Agencies (Miscellaneous Amendments) Regulations 2005 [s.8(2)].

Section 4 Care Standards Act 2000 (basic definitions) is amended by section 8(3) ACA 2002 to provide recognition of adoption support agencies and to ensure both Acts are compatible. The purpose of these provisions is to allow (properly regulated) agencies other than adoption agencies to provide support services, e.g. specialist birth records counselling and other services set out in the national framework.

REGULATIONS

Sections 9 and 10 contain regulation-making powers in respect of the adoption functions and management of local authorities, voluntary adoption agencies and adoption support agencies. Section 11 allows regulations to prescribe fees for certain services, including intercountry adoption.

Independent review of determinations [s.12 as amended by s.34 Children and Young Persons Act 2008]

Regulations under section 9 (the Independent Review of Determinations (Adoption and Fostering) Regulations 2009) establish a procedure under which any person in respect of whom a qualifying determination has been made by an adoption agency may apply to the appropriate Minister for a review of that determination [s.12.1].

A section 12(3A) is inserted so that regulations may impose a duty to pay to the appropriate Minister such sum as that Minister may determine and by virtue of section 12(3B), the appropriate Minster must secure that, taking one financial year with another, the aggregate of the sums which become payable to them under regulations made by virtue of section 12(3A) does not exceed the cost of performing the independent review functions.

The appropriate Minister may make an arrangement with an organisation under which independent review functions are performed by the organisation on their behalf [s.12(4)].

At the time of writing, the Independent Review Mechanism is provided by Coram Children's Legal Centre.

If the appropriate Minister makes such an arrangement (which may include payment to the organisation by the Minister), the organisation is to perform its functions in accordance with any general or special directions given by the appropriate Minister [s.12(5); (6)].

The Welsh Parliament is able to ask the English Secretary of State to provide its required independent review mechanism [s.12(7)].

At the time of writing, the Independent Review Mechanism Cymru is provided by Children in Wales.

In section 12, 'organisation' includes a public body and a private or voluntary organisation [s.12 (8)].

SUPPLEMENTAL

Information concerning adoption [ss.13–15]

Adoption agencies and courts are obliged to comply with directions from the appropriate Minister to provide statistical and other information relating to adoption [s.13].

Section 14 allows the appropriate Minister to exercise powers when a local authority has failed to comply with its duties under the Act or the Adoption (Intercountry Aspects) Act 1999.

Section 15 contains powers enabling the Minister to inspect premises or records.

Distribution of functions in relation to registered adoption societies [s.16]

Section 16 ACA 2002 inserts a new section 36A into Part 2 Care Standards Act 2000 which makes provision for the distribution of functions in relation to registered adoption societies.

Paragraph 106 of Schedule 3 dis-applies the requirement for separate branch registration in relation to registered adoption societies which will not therefore need to be separately registered.

Section 16(5) provides that the functions in relation to inspection are exercisable where the premises are in England, by Ofsted, and in Wales by the Assembly. Section 16(6) allows regulations to be made which will enable Ofsted to inspect branches of agencies operating in England but registered in Wales and vice versa.

Inquiries [s.17]

Section 17 was repealed by the Inquiries Act 2005 Schedule 3. Section 3 Children Act 2004 introduced the role of the Children's Commissioner in England and they are empowered to conduct inquiries into matters connected with the functions of an adoption agency if they consider that an individual case raises matters of public policy relevant to other children.

Such inquiries may be partly or wholly conducted in private.

Authorisation to place and consequences of placement

The following sections summarise the framework for placements and its:

- requirement that agencies must be 'authorised' to place a child; and
- establishment of two available routes for agency placement, i.e. placement with consent and placement by means of placement order.

PLACEMENT FOR ADOPTION BY ADOPTION AGENCY

Placement for adoption by adoption agency [s.18]

An adoption agency may:

- place a child for adoption with prospective adopters; or
- where it has placed a child with any persons, leave the child with them as prospective adopters [s.18(1)]; and
- except in the case of a child who is less than six weeks old, may only do so under section 19 or a placement order [s.18(1)].

An adoption agency may **only** place a child for adoption with prospective adopters if the agency is satisfied that the child ought to be placed for adoption [s.18(2)].

A child who is placed or authorised to be placed for adoption with prospective adopters by a local authority is looked after by the authority [s.18(3)].

If an application for an adoption order (including a Scottish or Northern Irish order) has been made by any persons in respect of a child and has not been disposed of:

- an adoption agency which placed the child with those persons, may leave the child with them until the application is disposed of; but
- apart from that, the child may not be placed for adoption with any prospective adopters [s.18(4)].

'Placing a child for adoption' includes where an agency has not placed a child with any persons, and is leaving the child with them as prospective adopters [s.18(5)].

An agency is 'authorised to place a child for adoption' where consent has been given under section 19 or the court has made a placement order [s.18(6)].

See Chapter 5 of the statutory guidance for detailed advice on placements.

Duty to consider Fostering for Adoption placement

Under section 22C (9A and 9B) of the Children Act 1989 as amended by the Children and Families Act 2014, where a local authority is considering adoption for a child or is satisfied that the child ought to be placed for adoption but is not yet authorised (either by consent or by placement order) to place the child for adoption, the authority MUST consider placing the child:

- with a relative, friend or other connected person who is also a local authority foster carer, or

- having decided that such a placement is not the most appropriate placement, with a local authority foster carer who has been approved as a prospective adopter. This may be a person who has dual approval as a foster carer and as an adopter, or an approved prospective adopter who has been temporarily approved as a foster carer for a named child under regulation 25A of the Care Planning, Placement and Case Review (England) Regulations 2010.

Placing children with parental consent [s.19]

The agency is authorised to place the child for adoption where an adoption agency is satisfied that each parent or guardian of a child has **consented** (and has not withdrawn the consent) to the child being placed for adoption with:

- prospective adopters identified in the consent; or

- any prospective adopters chosen by the agency [s.19(1)].

Consent to a child's placement with identified adopters may also include consent to a subsequent placement with **any** prospective adopters chosen by the agency if the first placement ends [s.19(2)].

Section 19(1) does not apply where:

- an application has been made on which a care order might be made and the application has not been disposed of; or

Authorisation to place and consequences of placement

- a care order or placement order has been made after the consent was given [s.19(3)].

References to a child placed for adoption under section 19 include a child who was placed under section 19 with prospective adopters and continues to be placed with them, whether or not consent to the placement has been withdrawn [s.19(4)].

This section is subject to section 52 (parental etc. consent) [s.19(5)].

Advance consent to adoption [s.20]

A parent or guardian of a child who consents to the child being placed for adoption by an adoption agency under section 19 may, at the same or any subsequent time, consent to the making of a future adoption order [s.20(1)].

Consent under section 20:

- where the parent or guardian has consented to the child being placed for adoption with prospective adopters identified in the consent, may be consent to adoption by them; or
- may be consent to adoption by any prospective adopters to be chosen by the agency [s.20(2)].

A person may withdraw any consent given under section 20 [s.20(3)].

A person who gives consent under section 20 may, at the same or any subsequent time, by notice given to the adoption agency:

- state that they do not wish to be informed of any application for an adoption order; or
- withdraw such a statement [s.20(4)].

'Notice' means written notice [s.144].

Witnessing consent [reg.20 Adoption Agencies Regulations 2005]

Regulation 20 requires agencies to request the appointment of a CAFCASS officer to witness consent to placement or future adoption

Authorisation to place and consequences of placement

under section 19 or section 20 of the Act, and to send the information specified in Schedule 2.

Where the person giving consent is outside England or Wales, regulation 20A deals with the procedure for witnessing consent.

Placement orders [s.21]

A placement order is an order made by the court authorising a local authority to place a child for adoption with any prospective adopters who may be chosen by the authority [s.21(1)].

The court may not make a placement order in respect of a child **unless** the child is subject to a care order, the court is satisfied the conditions in section 31(2) Children Act 1989 (conditions for making a care order) are met, or the child has no parent or guardian [s.21(2)] **and** the court is satisfied that each:

- parent or guardian has consented to the child being placed for adoption with any prospective adopters who may be chosen by the local authority and has not withdrawn the consent; or that the parent's or guardian's consent should be dispensed with [s.21(3)].

Section 21(3) is subject to section 52 (parental etc. consent).

A placement order continues in force until:

- it is revoked under section 24;
- an adoption order is made in respect of the child; or
- the child marries, enters into a civil partnership or attains the age of 18 years [s.21(4)].

Applications for placement orders [s.22]

A local authority **must** apply to the court for a placement order in respect of a child if:

- the child is placed for adoption by it, or is being provided with accommodation by it;

Authorisation to place and consequences of placement

- no adoption agency is authorised to place the child for adoption;
- the child has no parent or guardian or the authority considers that the conditions in section 31(2) Children Act 1989 are met; **and**
- the authority is satisfied that the child ought to be placed for adoption [s.22(1)].

The appropriate local authority must apply to the court for a placement order if it is satisfied that the child ought to be placed for adoption, and:

- an application has been made (and has not been disposed of) on which a care order might be made in respect of a child; or
- a child is subject to a care order and the appropriate local authority is not authorised to place the child for adoption [s.22(2)].

The authority **may** apply to the court for a placement order if:

- a child is subject to a care order; and
- the appropriate local authority is authorised to place the child for adoption under section 19 [s.22(3)].

Section 22(1) to (3) does not apply in respect of a child, if:

- any persons have given notice of intention to adopt, unless the period of four months beginning with the giving of the notice has expired without them applying for an adoption order or their application for such an order has been withdrawn or refused; or
- an application for an adoption order has been made and has not been disposed of [s.22(5)].

The court may give any directions it considers appropriate for medical or psychiatric examination or other assessment of the child (but a child who is of sufficient understanding to make an informed decision may refuse to submit to the examination or other assessment) where:

- an application for a placement order in respect of a child has been made and not been disposed of; and
- no interim care order is in force [s.22(6)].

Authorisation to place and consequences of placement

The appropriate local authority:

- in relation to a care order, is the local authority in whose care the child is placed by the order; and
- in relation to an application on which a care order might be made, is the local authority which makes the application [s.22(7)].

Varying placement orders [s.23]

The court may vary a placement order so as to substitute another local authority for the local authority authorised by the order to place the child for adoption [s.23(1)].

The variation may only be made on the joint application of both authorities [s.23(2)].

Revoking placement orders [s.24]

The court may revoke a placement order on the application of any person [s.24(1)].

But, someone other than the child or the local authority may apply only if:

- the court has given leave to apply; and
- the child is not placed for adoption by the authority [s.24(2)].

The court cannot give leave unless satisfied that there has been a change in circumstances since the order was made [s.24(3)].

If the court determines, on an application for an adoption order, not to make the order, it may revoke any placement order in respect of the child [s.24(4)].

The child may not, without the court's leave, be placed for adoption under the order, where:

- an application for revocation of a placement order has been made and has not been disposed of; and
- the child is not placed for adoption by the authority [s.24(5)].

Consequences of placement

Consent to placement or the making of a placement order has consequences for:

- parental responsibility;
- contact;
- surname and (more than temporary) removal from the UK.

These consequences are spelt out below and summarised in tabular form.

Parental responsibility [s.25]

If a child is placed for adoption under section 19, an adoption agency is authorised to place a child for adoption under that section, or a placement order is in force in respect of a child, parental responsibility for the child is given to the agency concerned [s.25(1); (2)].

While the child is placed with prospective adopters, parental responsibility is also given to them [s.25(3)].

The agency may determine that the parental responsibility of any parent or guardian, or of prospective adopters, should be restricted to the extent it decides is necessary [s.25(4)].

Contact [s.26]

On an adoption agency being authorised to place a child for adoption, or upon placing a child for adoption who is less than six weeks old, any provision for contact under the Children Act 1989 Act ceases to have effect [s.26(1)].

While an adoption agency is so authorised, or a child is placed for adoption:

- no application may be made for any contact provision under the Children Act 1989; but
- the court may make an order under section 26 requiring the person with whom the child lives, or is to live, to allow them to visit or stay with the person named in the order, or for the person named in the order and the child to have contact with each other [s.26(2)].

An application for an order under section 26 may be made by:

- the child or agency;
- any parent, guardian or relative;
- any person in whose favour there was provision for contact under the Children Act 1989 which ceased to have effect by virtue of section 26(1);
- if a child arrangements order was in force immediately before the adoption agency was authorised to place the child for adoption (or placed the child for adoption at a time when they were less than six weeks old), the person in whose favour the order was made;
- another individual if they had care of the child immediately before that time by virtue of an order made in the exercise of the High Court's inherent jurisdiction with respect to children;
- any person who has obtained the court's leave to make the application [s.26(3)].

When making a placement order, the court may on its own initiative make an order under section 26 [s.26(4)].

Section 26 does not prevent an application for a contact order under section 8 Children Act 1989 being made where the application is to be heard together with an application for an adoption order in respect of the child [s.26(5)].

In section 26, 'provision for contact under the 1989 Act' means a child arrangements order under section 8 or an order under section 34 of that Act (parental contact with children in care) [s.26(6)].

Consequences of placement

Contact: supplementary [s.27]

An order under section 26:

- has effect while the adoption agency is authorised to place the child for adoption or the child is placed for adoption; but
- may be varied or revoked by the court on an application by the child, the agency or a person named in the order [s.27(1)].

The agency may refuse to allow contact that would otherwise be required by a section 26 order if:

- it is satisfied that it is necessary to do so in order to safeguard or promote the child's welfare; and
- refusal is decided upon as a matter of urgency and does not last for more than seven days [s.27(2)].

Regulation 47 of the Adoption Agency Regulations 2005 specifies the:

- steps to be taken by an agency which has exercised its power under section 27(2);
- circumstances in which, and conditions subject to which, terms of any order under section 26 may be departed from by agreement between the agency and any person for whose contact with the child the order provides;
- notification by an agency of any variation or suspension of arrangements made (other than under an order under section 26) with a view to allowing any person contact with the child [s.27(3)].

Before making a placement order, the court must:

- consider the arrangements which the adoption agency has made, or proposes to make, for allowing any person contact with the child; and
- invite the parties to the proceedings to comment [s.27(4)].

An order under section 26 may provide for contact on any conditions the court considers appropriate [s.27(5)].

Further consequences of placement [s.28]

Where a child has been placed with parental consent or an adoption agency is authorised to place a child for adoption under section 19:

- a parent or guardian of the child may **not** apply for a 'live with' child arrangements order unless an application for an adoption order has been made and they have obtained the court's leave under section 47(3) or (5);

- if an application has been made for an adoption order, a guardian of the child may not apply for a special guardianship order unless they have obtained the court's leave under section 47(3) or (5) [s.28(1)].

Where a child is placed for adoption or an adoption agency is authorised to place a child for adoption under section 19, or a placement order is in force in respect of them, then (whether or not they are in England and Wales) a person may **not**, unless the court gives leave, or each parent or guardian of the child gives written consent [s.28(2)]:

- cause the child to be known by a new surname; or
- remove the child from the UK [s.28(2); (3)].

Section 28(3) does not prevent the removal of a child from the UK for a period of less than one month by a person who provides the child's home.

Further consequences of placement orders [s.29]

Where a placement order is made in respect of a child and either the child is subject to a care order, or the court at the same time makes a care order in respect of the child, the care order does not have effect at any time when the placement order is in force [s.29(1)].

On the making of a placement order in respect of a child, any order mentioned in section 8(1) Children Act 1989 and any supervision order in respect of the child, ceases to have effect [s.29(2)].

Consequences of placement

Where a placement order is in force, the following orders may **not** be made in respect of the child:

- prohibited steps order, child arrangements order or specific issue order;
- supervision or child assessment order [s.29(3)].

The first of the above two prohibitions does not apply in respect of a 'live with' child arrangements order if:

- an application for an adoption order has been made in respect of the child; and
- the child arrangements order is applied for by a parent or guardian who has obtained the court's leave under section 47(3) or (5) or by any other person who has obtained the court's leave under this subsection [s.29(4)].

Where a placement order is in force, no special guardianship order may be made in respect of the child unless:

- an application has been made for an adoption order; and
- the person applying for the special guardianship order has obtained the court's leave under section 29(5) or, if they are a guardian of the child, has obtained the court's leave under section 47(5) [s.29(5)].

A person who has 'leave to apply' is not required to give three months' notice of their application for a special guardianship order as otherwise required by section 14A(7) Children Act 1989 [s.29(6)].

Where a placement order is in force, a special guardian with whom the child lives is permitted to take the child out of the UK for a period of up to one month.

Summary of placement routes and their consequences

ROUTE TO PLACEMENT	CONSEQUENCES
Consent (s.19)	Agency is given parental responsibility and can restrict parents' exercise of their responsibility.
	Any Children Act 1989 provisions for contact cease and will be dealt with under sections 26 & 27.
	In case of a local authority, the child is looked after though some 'looked after children' regulations will not apply.
	Without written consent of each parent/guardian or the Consequences of placement court's permission, nobody may change the child's surname or remove them from the UK (for a month or more).
	Parent or guardian may withdraw consent up to lodging of adoption order application.
	Once placed, prospective adopters have parental responsibility (may be restricted by the agency) and parent or guardian may not apply for a child arrangements order (except with court's permission, within adoption application).
	Parent is not permitted to oppose the grant of an adoption order unless the court grants permission (and it can do so only if satisfied there has been a change of circumstances).
Placement order (s.21)	In addition to the above consequences:
	Any care order in force is suspended for the duration of the placement order.

> Any Children Act 1989 section 8 or supervision order ceases to have effect.
>
> No Children Act 1989 section 8, supervision, child assessment or special guardianship order may be applied for (except, within the adoption application, the court may give permission for making of an application for a child arrangements order or special guardianship order).
>
> Placement orders cease when the child is adopted, reaches 18 or is married or has a civil partnership.
>
> They can be revoked on an application to court but only the local authority or the child may apply without leave – others can apply only with the court's permission (which cannot be given if the child has been placed for adoption) and only if the court is satisfied there has been a change of circumstances.

Removal of children who are or may be placed by adoption agencies

The ACA 2002 introduced measures to ensure children placed for adoption are not precipitately removed.

The measures distinguish between agency and non-agency cases.

Key points are that:

- the agency acts as a go-between and if the child is placed with prospective adopters, only the agency may remove them;

- even where the parent has a right to the return of the child, seven or 14 days are allowed (according to circumstances) for negotiation and preparation of the child;
- there are criminal sanctions for removing a child contrary to, or failing to return a child to the agency in accordance with, the law (and recovery orders may be made against those who fail to comply);
- the making of an application for a placement order has the effect of barring a child's removal from local authority accommodation without leave;
- where the child is subject to a care order, the Children Act 1989 provisions apply in place of sections 31–33 of this Act;
- these provisions do not prevent the removal of a child who is arrested nor the exercise of local authority or other powers apart from the right of a parent to remove their child from local authority accommodation under section 20 Children Act 1989, i.e. an emergency protection order or use of police powers of protection remain possible. A local authority may also remove a child in the exercise of their power to decide a child's placement under a placement order.

Recovery by parents etc where child not placed or is a baby [s.31]

Section 31(2) applies where:

- the child is not yet placed for adoption but section 19 consent was given (even if subsequently withdrawn);
- a baby under six weeks old was placed and remains with prospective adopters (without consent under section 19) even if they are now more than six weeks old.

In these circumstances, if the parent informs the agency that they wish the child to be returned to them, the agency must return the child within seven days, unless it applies or has applied for a placement order.

Where the child is actually placed, the agency must give notice to the prospective adopters who must return the child to the agency within seven days. The agency must then immediately return the child to the parent.

If the prospective adopters fail to comply, the parent is not permitted in consequence of section 30(1) to remove their child. In such circumstances, the agency or parent may apply for a section 41 recovery order (see below).

It is the application for a placement order that effectively freezes a parent's right to have their child returned.

Recovery by parents etc where child placed and consent withdrawn [s.32]

Section 32 applies where a child is placed for adoption by an adoption agency following consent to placement under section 19 and that consent has been withdrawn.

Withdrawal of consent after an application for adoption has been issued is ineffective.

Unless an application is or has been made for a placement order, the agency must give the prospective adopters notice and they must return the child to the agency within 14 days and the agency must then immediately return the child to their parent.

If before notice is given to the prospective adopters, an application for an adoption order, special guardianship order or child arrangements order (or for leave to apply for a special guardianship order or child arrangements order) has been made in respect of the child, the prospective adopters will not be required to return the child unless the court so orders [s.32(5)].

Regulation 38 of the Adoption Agencies Regulations 2005 indicates that when consent is withdrawn, a local authority must immediately review its decision to place a child for adoption and consider whether to apply for a placement order.

In the case of a voluntary agency, it must immediately inform the local authority where the child is living.

Birth parents need to be advised that if they were to withdraw consent to placement but did not inform the agency that they wanted the child returned, the prospective adopters might issue an adoption (or other) application before any notice was served on them. It would then be for the court to decide whether to order the child's return.

Recovery by parents etc where child placed and placement order refused [s.33]

Section 33 applies where a child was placed for adoption by a local authority under section 19 and the local authority is unsuccessful in an application for a placement order.

Where the parent requests the return of the child, the court will fix a date for the prospective adopters to return the child to the local authority, at which time it must return the child to their parents.

Placement orders: prohibition on removal [s.34]

Section 34 prohibits the removal of a child while a placement order is in force and also restricts the ability of a parent or anyone else to remove the child when the placement order is revoked.

The return of the child to the parent is a matter to be determined by the court.

If the child is actually placed with prospective adopters at the time of revocation, the court will determine whether/when the child is to be returned by the former prospective adopters to the local authority.

Return of child in other cases [s.35]

This section deals with placement disruptions that are independent of any action or notice by birth parents.

Prospective adopters may give the agency notice of their wish to return the child and the agency may give notice to the prospective adopters that, in its opinion, the child should not remain with them.

In either case:

- the child is to be returned to and received by the agency within seven days of the notice;
- the agency must inform the parent/guardian.

The latter requirement is significant, especially when a placement order exists, since the parent can only apply for revocation of a placement order if the child is not placed for adoption.

Regulation 36 of the Adoption Agencies Regulations 2005 requires the local authority to review (28 to 42 days following the disruption) the case of a child returned by prospective adopters.

Removal of children in non-agency case

Restrictions on removal [s.36]

This section places restrictions on the removal of a child from prospective adopters who have:

- applied for an adoption order (while the application is pending);
- given notice of intention to adopt; or
- applied for leave to apply for an adoption order under section 42(6).

In general, the court's leave will be required to remove the child except where the person concerned is acting under statutory powers (other than a parent's right under section 20 Children Act 1989 to remove their child from local authority accommodation).

There are two exceptions:

- foster carer cases;
- step-parent cases.

If local authority **foster carers** give notice of their intention to adopt a child whom they have been looking after for more than one year but less than five years, the person with parental responsibility may exercise the power to remove the child under section 20(8) Children Act 1989 without the court's leave.

In the case of **step-parents**, where the partner of a parent has given notice of intention to adopt a child who has had their home with that partner for less than three out of the last five years, a parent or guardian may remove the child without the court's leave.

The above right would not be subject to any restrictions that might apply if the other parent had a child arrangements order in their favour.

Applicants for adoption [s.37]

At any time when a child is living with anyone with whom they are not placed by an adoption agency, but those people have applied for an adoption order and the application is pending, the following may remove the child:

- a person who has the court's leave;
- a local authority or other person in the exercise of a power conferred by any law (except section 20(8) Children Act 1989 – removal of a child from accommodation [s.37(1)].

Local authority foster carers [s.38]

Section 38 applies if the child is living with local authority foster carers.

If the child has lived with the foster carers at all times in the five years before their removal and the foster carers have given notice of intention to adopt, or an application has been made for leave under section 42(6) and is still pending, the following may remove the child:

- a person who has the court's leave;

- a local authority or other person in the exercise of a power conferred by any law – other than section 20(8) Children Act 1989 [s.38(2) & (3)].

If the child has lived with the foster carers at all times in the one year before removal, and the foster carers have given notice of intention to adopt, the following may remove the child:

- a person with parental responsibility for the child who is exercising the power in section 20(8) Children Act 1989;
- a person who has the court's leave;
- a local authority or other person in the exercise of a power conferred by any law, other than section 20(8) Children Act 1989 [s.38(5)].

Partners of parents [s.39]

Section 39 applies if a child lives with a partner of a parent and that partner has given notice of intention to adopt [s.39(1)].

If the child has lived with the partner for not less than three years (continuous or not) during the five years before removal, the following may remove the child:

- a person who has the court's leave;
- a local authority or other person in the exercise of a power conferred by any law, other than section 20(8) Children Act 1989 [s.39(2)].

In other cases where the partner has given notice of intention to adopt, the child may be removed by a:

- parent or guardian;
- person who has the court's leave;
- local authority or other person in the exercise of a power conferred by any enactment, other than section 20(8) Children Act 1989 [s.39(3)].

Other non-agency cases [s.40]

In other non-agency cases, so long as the persons concerned have given notice of intention to adopt, or applied for leave and the application is pending, the following may remove the child:

- a person who has the court's leave;
- a local authority or other person in the exercise of a power conferred by any law (other than section 20(8) Children Act 1989).

BREACH OF RESTRICTIONS ON REMOVAL

Recovery orders [s.41]

Where it appears to the court that a child has been unlawfully removed or there are reasonable grounds for believing that a person intends to unlawfully remove a child, or has failed to comply with requirements related to removal or return, the court may, on the application of any person, by an order:

- direct any person who can to produce the child on request to a specified person;
- authorise removal of the child by a specified person;
- require any person who has information about the child's whereabouts to disclose it on request to the police or a court officer;
- authorise the police to enter any premises specified in the order and search for the child, using reasonable force if necessary.

The persons who may be specified are:

- a person named by the court;
- the police;
- a person authorised by the adoption agency that is authorised to place the child for adoption.

A person who intentionally obstructs a person exercising such a power of removal conferred by the order is guilty of an offence.

Adoption orders

The following section outlines some 'pre-conditions' for making adoption orders:

- child to live with adopter;
- agency court report on suitability of applicant/s;
- a notice of intention to adopt;
- suitability of adopters.

The section also defines and includes conditions for the making of an adoption order that are related to:

- parental consent;
- child's placement for adoption with the prospective adopters;
- child's status as 'freed for adoption' (under Scottish/Northern Irish law);
- age and marital status of child;
- any previous application;
- age and parental status of the applicant/s.

PRELIMINARIES TO ADOPTION

Child to live with adopters before application made [s.42]

An application for an adoption order may not be made unless specified conditions (that vary according to the child's circumstances) are met.

If the child was placed for adoption with the applicant/s by an adoption agency or in pursuance of an order of the High Court, or the applicant is a parent of the child:

- the condition is they must have lived with one or other or both applicant/s at all times during the ten weeks preceding the application [s.42(2)].

If the applicant or one of the applicants is the partner of a parent of the child, the condition is that the child must have lived with the applicant/s at all times during the period of six months preceding the application [s.42(3)].

If the applicants are local authority foster carers, the condition is that the child must have lived with the applicants at all times during the one year preceding the application [s.42(4)].

In cases where a British resident has complied with the relevant requirement and brought a child into the UK for the purposes of adoption, regulation 9 of the Adoptions with a Foreign Element Regulations 2005 requires that the child must have lived with the applicant/s for not less than six months preceding the application.

In case where a British resident has not complied with the relevant requirement, the residence requirement is extended to 12 months.

In any other case, the condition is the child must have lived with the applicant or, in the case of an application by a couple, with one or both of them for not less than three years (continuous or not) during the five years preceding the application [s.42(5)].

Sections 42(4) and (5) do not prevent an application being made if the court gives leave to make it [s.42(6)].

An adoption order may not be made unless the court is satisfied that sufficient opportunities to see the child at home together with the applicant/s have been given to the adoption agency/local authority.

Reports where child placed by agency [s.43]

Where an application for an adoption order relates to a child placed for adoption by an adoption agency, the agency must:

- submit to the court a report on the suitability of applicants and any other matters relevant to the operation of section 1, and

- assist the court in any manner the court directs.

Notice of intention to adopt [s.44]

Where a child has not been placed for adoption by an adoption agency, an adoption order may not be made in respect of them unless the proposed adopters have given notice to the appropriate local authority of their intention to apply for the order [s.44(2)].

The notice must be given not more than two years, or less than three months, before the date on which the application for the adoption order is made [s.44(3)].

Any carers who require the court's leave to reply may not issue a notice until they have the court's leave to apply [s.44(4)].

On receipt of a notice of intention to adopt, the local authority must arrange for the investigation of the matter and submit to the court a report of the investigation [s.44(5)].

In particular, the investigation must, so far as is practicable, include the suitability of the proposed adopters and any other matters relevant to the operation of section 1 in relation to the application [s.44(6)].

If a local authority receives a notice of intention to adopt in respect of a child whom it knows was (immediately before the notice was given) looked after by another local authority, it must, within seven days, inform the other local authority [s.44(7)].

The authority is not to be treated as leaving the child with carers as prospective adopters for the purposes of section 18(1)(b), where:

- a local authority has placed a child with any persons otherwise than as prospective adopters; and
- the persons give notice of intention to adopt [s.44(8)].

In section 44, the appropriate local authority is the authority where, at the time of the notice, the proposed adopters have their home. If they do not have a home in England and Wales, the Local Authority

(Adoption (Miscellaneous Provisions)) Regulations 2005 make provision as to the relevant local authority.

Suitability of adopters [s.45]

The Suitability of Adopters Regulations 2005 issued under section 9 make provision as to the matters to be taken into account by an adoption agency in determining, or making any report in respect of, the suitability of any persons to adopt a child, and in particular, in the case of a couple, proper regard to the need for stability and permanence in their relationship [s.45(1); (2)].

THE MAKING OF ADOPTION ORDERS

Making adoption orders [s.46]

An adoption order is an order made by the court on an application under section 50 or 51 giving parental responsibility for a child to the adopter/s [s.46(1)].

The making of an adoption order operates to extinguish:

- the parental responsibility which any person other than the adopters or adopter has for the adopted child immediately before the making of the order;

- any order under the 1989 Act or the Children (Northern Ireland) Order 1995;

- any order under the Children (Scotland) Act 1995 other than an excepted order; and

- any duty arising by virtue of an agreement or order of a court to make payments, so far as payments are in respect of the adopted child's maintenance or upbringing for any period after the making of the adoption order except for an agreement which constitutes a trust, or expressly provides that the duty is not to be extinguished by the making of an adoption order [s.46(2); (4)].

'Excepted order' means an order under sections 9, 11(1)(d) or 13 Children (Scotland) Act 1995 or an exclusion order within the meaning of section 76(1) of that Act.

Section 46(3)(b) preserves the parental status of a parent whose partner obtains an adoption order in respect of their child.

An adoption order may be made even if the child to be adopted is already an adopted child [s.46(5)].

Before making an adoption order, the court must consider whether there should be arrangements for allowing any person contact with the child, and for that purpose the court must consider any existing or proposed arrangements and obtain any views of the parties to the proceedings [s.46(6)].

Conditions of making adoption orders [s.47]

If a child has a parent or guardian, an adoption order may not be made unless one of the three conditions described below is met (though section 47 is subject to section 52 – parental etc. consent) [s.47(1)].

The conditions are related to:

- consent
- placement
- the child being freed for adoption (Northern Ireland only)
- the child being subject to a relevant Scottish permanence order.

The **first condition** is that, in the case of each parent or guardian, the court is satisfied that:

- the parent or guardian consents to the making of the adoption order;
- the parent or guardian has consented under section 20 (and has not withdrawn the consent) and does not oppose the making of the adoption order; or

Adoption orders

- the parent's or guardian's consent should be dispensed with [s.47(2)].

Where they have given advance consent under section 20, a parent or guardian may not oppose the making of an adoption order without the court's leave [s.47(3)].

The **second condition** is that:

- the child has been placed for adoption by an adoption agency, with the prospective adopters in whose favour the order is proposed to be made and;
- **either**, the child was placed for adoption with the consent of each parent or guardian and the consent of the mother was given when the child was at least six weeks old, **or** the child was placed for adoption under a placement order; and
- no parent or guardian opposes the making of the adoption order [s.47(4)].

All three of the above conditions must be met to the satisfaction of the court.

A parent or guardian may not oppose the making of an adoption order under this second condition without the court's leave [s.47(5)].

The **third condition** is that the child is free for adoption by virtue of an order made:

- in Scotland, under section 18 of the Adoption (Scotland) Act 1978 [see also section 80 of the Adoption & Children (Scotland) Act 2007 or a deemed permanence order]
- in Northern Ireland, under Article 17(1) or 18(1) of Adoption (Northern Ireland) Order 1987 (S.I.1987/2203 (N.I.22) [s.47(6)].

The court cannot give leave under section 47(3) or (5) unless satisfied that there has been a change in circumstances since the consent of the parent or guardian was given or, as the case may be, the placement order was made [s.47(7)].

An adoption order may not be made in relation to a person who is or has been married [s.47(8)] or who is or has been a civil partner [s.47(8A)].

An adoption order may not be made in relation to a person who has attained the age of 19 years [s.47(9)].

Restrictions on making adoption orders [s.48]

The court may **not** hear an application for an adoption order, where a previous application for an adoption order in the UK, Isle of Man or any of the Channel Islands, made in relation to the child by the same persons was refused by any court, **unless** it appears to the court that, because of a change in circumstances or for any other reason, it is proper to hear the application.

Applications for adoption: residence requirement [s.49]

Useful advice on domicile and habitual residence is given in Guidance [3.2–3.5].

A **single** applicant must be domiciled in a part of the British Islands or have been habitually resident there for at least a year preceding the application.

In the case of a **couple**, either both must have been habitually resident in a part of the British Islands for at least a year preceding the application or one of them must be domiciled there.

Applications for adoption: age requirements [ss.49, 50, 51]

Applicants for an adoption order must be at least 21 years of age except that a parent adopting their own child with their partner may be aged 18 to 20 [s.50(2)].

References in the ACA 2002 to a child, in connection with any proceedings (whether or not concluded) for adoption, e.g. 'child to be adopted' or 'adopted child' include a person who has attained the age of 18 years before the proceedings are concluded [s.49(5)].

Adoption by a couple [s.50]

An application may be made by a couple defined in section 144(4) as:

- a married couple;
- civil partners;
- two people (of different or the same sex) living as partners in an enduring family relationship – other than parent, grandparent, sibling, aunt or uncle.

Adoption by one person [s.51]

An application can be made by one person if they are:

- unmarried and has not entered into a registered civil partnership;
- living as the partner of the parent of the child;
- married or has entered into a civil partnership which has not been dissolved and their spouse cannot be found/they have separated and the separation is likely to be permanent/the spouse/partner is by reason of ill-health incapable of making an application; or if
- this is an adoption order that may not be made to the child's parent alone unless the other parent is dead or cannot be found, or there is no other parent or there is some other reason justifying the adoption by one parent alone [s.51(4)].

PLACEMENT AND ADOPTION: GENERAL

Parental etc. consent [s.52]

The court cannot dispense with parental consent to the child being placed for adoption or to the making of an adoption order unless satisfied that:

- the parent or guardian cannot be found or is incapable of giving consent; or
- the welfare of the child requires the consent to be dispensed with [s.52(1)].

'Consent' means consent given unconditionally and with full understanding of what is involved; but a person may consent to adoption without knowing the identity of the persons in whose favour the order will be made [s.52(5)].

Any consent given by the mother to the making of an adoption order is ineffective if it is given fewer than six weeks after her child's birth [s.52(3)].

'Parent', except in section 52(9) and section 52(10) below means a parent having parental responsibility.

The withdrawal of any consent to the placement of a child for adoption, or of any consent given under section 20 is ineffective if it is given after an application for an adoption order is made [s.52(4)].

Consent must be given in the form prescribed by the Family Procedure Rules 2010 (Rule 14.10) and any withdrawal of consent must also be in the form prescribed by rules, or by notice given to the agency [s.52(7); (8)].

If an agency has placed a child for adoption under section 19 in pursuance of consent given by a parent of the child, and later, the other parent of the child acquires parental responsibility for the child:

- the other parent is to be treated as though they had given consent in the same terms in accordance with section 52 [s.52(9); (10)].

Modification of 1989 Act in relation to adoption [s.53]

Section 53 permits provisions in the Children Act 1989 to be modified in respect of children awaiting adoption – see regulation 45 Adoption Agencies Regulations.

Where a child is living with persons who have given notice of intention to adopt, the child's parents are not liable to pay any contributions towards the maintenance of children looked after by local authorities [Adoption Agencies Regulations 45(2)(d)] from the time they provide notice until:

- four months thereafter; or

Disclosure of information

- an application for such an order is withdrawn or refused [s.53(5)].

Disclosing information during adoption process [s.54]

Regulations under section 9 may require adoption agencies in prescribed circumstances to disclose in accordance with the regulations prescribed information to prospective adopters [s.54].

Disclosure of information

DISCLOSURE OF INFORMATION IN RELATION TO A PERSON'S ADOPTION

Information to be kept about a person's adoption [s.56]

The Disclosure of Adoption Information (Post-Commencement Adoptions) Regulations 2005 prescribe the:

- information which an adoption agency must keep in relation to a person's adoption;
- form and manner in which it must keep that information;
- arrangements for transfer of information to another adoption agency [s.56(1); (3)].

Any information kept by an adoption agency by virtue of section 56(1) responsibility (information the agency must keep in relation to a person's adoption) is referred to as 'section 56 information' [s.56(2)].

Restrictions on disclosure of protected etc information [s.57]

The information to which a person is restricted by virtue of section 57(1) or (2) is referred to as 'protected information' [s.57(3)].

'Identifying information' about a person means information that on its own or together with other information disclosed by an adoption agency, identifies the person or enables the person to be identified [s.57(4)].

Disclosure of information

Any 'section 56 information' kept by an adoption agency which is about an adopted or any other person and is or includes identifying information about the person may **only** be disclosed to a person (other than the person the information is about) in accordance with sections 57–65 below [s.57(1)].

Any information kept by an adoption agency that the agency has obtained from the Registrar General and any other information that would enable the adopted person to obtain a certified copy of their birth certificate, or about an entry relating to them in the Adoption Contact Register, may only be disclosed to a person by the agency in pursuance of sections 57–65 [s.57(2)].

Section 57 does not prevent the disclosure of protected information in pursuance of a prescribed agreement to which the adoption agency is a party [s.57(5)].

Part 3 of the Disclosure of Adoption Information (Post-Commencement Adoptions) Regulations 2005 in defined circumstances authorises an adoption agency to disclose protected information to a person who is not an adopted person [s.57(6)].

Disclosure of other information [s.58]

Section 58 applies to any section 56 information other than protected information [s.58(1)].

An adoption agency may, for purposes of its functions, disclose to any person in accordance with prescribed arrangements any information to which section 58 applies [s.58(1)].

An adoption agency must, in prescribed circumstances, disclose prescribed information to a prescribed person [s.58(2)].

Offence [s.59]

Regulation 21 of the Disclosure of Adoption Information (Post-Commencement Adoptions) Regulations 2005 provides that a registered adoption society which discloses any information in contravention of

Disclosure of information

section 57 is guilty of an offence and liable on summary conviction to a fine not exceeding level 5 on the standard scale [s.59(1)].

Disclosing information to adopted adult [s.60]

Section 60 applies to an adopted person who has attained the age of 18 years [s.60(1)].

The adopted person has the right, at their request, to receive from the appropriate adoption agency, any:

- information which would enable them to obtain a certified copy of the record of their birth, unless the High Court orders otherwise;
- prescribed information disclosed to the adopters by the agency by virtue of section 54 [s.60(2)].

The High Court may make an order under the former of the two section 60(2) provisions, on an application by the appropriate adoption agency, if satisfied that the circumstances are exceptional [s.60(3)].

The adopted person also has the right, at their request, to receive from the court which made the adoption order a copy of any prescribed document or prescribed order relating to the adoption [s.60(4)].

Section 60(4) does not apply to a document or order so far as it contains information which is protected information [s.60(5)].

Disclosing protected information about adults [s.61]

Section 61 applies where:

- a person applies to the appropriate adoption agency for protected information to be disclosed to them; and
- **none** of the information is about a person who is a child at the time of the application [s.61(1)].

The agency is not required to proceed with the application unless it considers it appropriate to do so [s.61(2)].

Disclosure of information

If the agency does proceed, it must take all reasonable steps to obtain the views of any person the information is about as to the disclosure of the information [s.61(3)].

The agency may then disclose the information if it considers it appropriate to do so [s.61(4)].

In deciding if it is appropriate to proceed with the application or disclose the information, the agency must consider:

- the welfare of the adopted person;
- any views obtained under section 61(3);
- any prescribed matters;
- and all other circumstances of the case [s.61(5)].

Sections 61 and 62 do not apply to a request by the adopted person for information to enable a certified copy of their birth certificate, to prescribed information disclosed to their adopters nor to the disclosure of protected information to a person who is not adopted [s.61(6)].

Disclosing protected information about children [s.62]

Section 62 applies where:

- a person applies to the appropriate adoption agency for protected information to be disclosed to them; and
- **any** of the information is about a person who is a child at the time of the application [s.62(1)].

The agency is not required to proceed with the application unless it considers it appropriate to do so and if it does proceed, then, so far as the information is about a child, the agency must take all reasonable steps to obtain, the views of:

- any parent or guardian of the child; and
- the child, if the agency considers it appropriate to do so having regard to their age and understanding and to all the other circumstances of the case [s.62(2); (3)].

Disclosure of information

So far as the information is about a person who has at the time attained the age of 18 years, the agency must take all reasonable steps to obtain their views as to the disclosure of the information [s.62(4)].

The agency may then disclose the information if it considers it appropriate to do so [s.62(5)].

In deciding if it is appropriate to proceed with the application, or disclose the information, where any of the information is about a person who is at the time a child:

- if the child is an adopted child, the child's welfare must be the paramount consideration;
- in the case of any other child, the agency must have particular regard to the child's welfare [s.62(6)].

In deciding whether it is appropriate to proceed with the application or disclose the information, the agency must consider the welfare of the adopted person (when they are not a child), any views obtained under section 62(3) or (4), any prescribed matters and all the other circumstances of the case [s.62(7)].

Counselling [s.63]

Part 5 of the Disclosure of Adoption Information (Post-Commencement Adoptions) Regulations requires adoption agencies to give information about availability of counselling to persons:

- seeking information from them;
- considering objecting or consenting to the disclosure of information by the agency in pursuance of this group of sections; or
- considering entering with the agency into an agreement [s.63(1)].

Other provision to be made by regulations [s.64]

The Disclosure of Adoption Information (Post-Commencement Adoptions) Regulations 2005 make detailed provision for the purposes of sections 57–65 (disclosure of information).

Status of adopted children

Meaning of adoption [s.66]

In sections 66–76 'adoption' means (and related expressions should be interpreted accordingly):

- adoption by an adoption order or a Scottish or Northern Irish adoption order;
- adoption by an order made in the Isle of Man or any of the Channel Islands;
- an adoption effected under the law of a Convention country outside the British Islands, certified in pursuance of Article 23(1) of the Convention (referred to as a 'Convention adoption');
- an overseas adoption (section 87); or
- an adoption recognised by the law of England and Wales and effected under the law of any other country [s.66(1)].

References in sections 66–76 to 'adoption' exclude pre-commencement adoptions [s.66(2)].

Any reference in an enactment to an adopted person within the meaning of these sections includes a reference to an adopted child within the meaning of Part 4 Adoption Act 1976 (this part of the 1976 Act being preserved by Sch. 5 of this Act) [s.66(3)].

Status conferred by adoption [s.67]

An adopted person is to be treated in law as if born to the adopter/s [s.67(1)].

An adopted person is the **legitimate** child of the adopter/s and must be treated as their child if adopted by:

- a couple; or

Status of adopted children

- one of a couple under section 51(2) – i.e. where the person has attained 21 and is the partner of the parent of the child [s.67(2)].

If adopted by one member of a couple under section 51(2), a child must be treated in law as **their** child (though this does not affect any reference in this Act to their natural parent or other natural relationship) [s.67(3)(a)].

In any other case, section 67(3)(b) provides that an adopted person must in law be treated **only** as the child of the adopter/s, though once again this does not affect any reference in this Act to a child's natural parent or other natural relationship.

Where an adopter is a sole adopter **and** the natural parent, section 67(3)(b) has no effect with respect to anything that depends upon the child's relationship to that parent, e.g. entitlement to property [s.67(4)].

Section 67 takes effect from the date of the adoption [s.67(5)].

Adoptive relatives [s.68]

A relationship existing by virtue of section 67 may be referred to as an adoptive relationship, and:

- an adopter may be referred to as an adoptive parent/adoptive father/adoptive mother;
- any other relative of any degree under an adoptive relationship may be referred to as an adoptive relative of that degree [s.68(1)].

If the child was adopted by a couple of the same sex, or a partner of the child's parent, where the couple are of the same sex:

- a reference to the adoptive 'mother' and 'father' of a child is to be read as a reference to the child's adoptive parents [s.68(3)].

The Registers

ADOPTED CHILDREN REGISTER

Adoptive relatives [s.77]

The Registrar General must maintain the 'Adopted Children Register' which is not open to public inspection or search [s.77(1); (2)].

No entries may be made in the Adopted Children Register other than entries:

- directed to be made in it by adoption orders; or
- required to be made under Schedule 1 [s.77(3)].

A certified copy of an entry in the Register, if purporting to be sealed or stamped with the seal of the General Register Office, is sufficient evidence of the adoption to which it relates [s.77(4)].

Where an entry in the Register contains a record of the date of birth, country, or district and sub-district, of the birth of the adopted person:

- a certified copy of the entry is also sufficient evidence in all respects as if the copy were a certified copy of an entry in the registers of live births [s.77(5)].

Searches and copies [s.78]

The Registrar General must continue to maintain an index of the Adopted Children Register [s.78(1)].

Any person may:

- search the index;
- have a certified copy of any entry in the Adopted Children Register [s.78(2)].

A person is not entitled to have a certified copy of an entry in that Register relating to an adopted person who has not attained the age of

18 years unless they have provided the Registrar General with the prescribed particulars.

'Prescribed' means prescribed by regulations (the Adopted Children and Adoption Contact Register Regulations 2005) made by the Registrar General with the approval of the Chancellor of the Exchequer [s.78(3)].

Connection between the register and birth records [s.79]

The Registrar General must make traceable the connection between any entry in the registers of live births or other records which has been marked 'Adopted' and any corresponding entry in the Adopted Children Register [s.79(1)].

Information kept by the Registrar General for the above is not open to public inspection or search [s.79(2)].

Any such information, and any other information which would enable an adopted person to obtain a certified copy of the record of their birth, may **only** be disclosed by the Registrar General in accordance with section 79 [s.79(3)].

In relation to a person adopted before 30.12.05 the court may, in exceptional circumstances, order the Registrar General to give any information mentioned in section 79(3) to a person [s.79(4)].

On an application made in the prescribed manner by the appropriate adoption agency in respect of an adopted person a record of whose birth is kept by the Registrar General, the Registrar General must give the agency any information relating to the adopted person which is mentioned in section 79(3) [s.79(5)].

'Appropriate adoption agency' has the same meaning as in section 65. In relation to a person adopted before 30.12.05, Schedule 2 applies instead of section 79(5).

On an application made in the prescribed manner by an adopted person a record of whose birth is kept by the Registrar General and who is under the age of 18 years, and intends to be married:

- the Registrar General must inform the applicant if it appears from information contained in the registers of live births or other records that the applicant and the person whom the applicant intends to marry may be within the prohibited degrees of relationship for the purposes of the Marriage Act 1949 [s.79(7)].

Before the Registrar General gives any information by virtue of this section, any prescribed fee which they have demanded must be paid [s.79(8)].

ADOPTION CONTACT REGISTER

Adoption contact register [s.80]

The Registrar General must continue to maintain at the General Register Office in accordance with regulations a register in two parts, to be called the 'Adoption Contact Register' [s.80(1)].

Part 1 of the register is to contain information about adopted persons who have given notice expressing their wishes as to making contact with their relatives [s.80(2)].

The Registrar General may only make an entry in Part 1 of the register for an adopted person who:

- has a birth record kept by the Registrar General;
- has attained the age of 18 years; and
- who the Registrar General is satisfied has such information as is necessary to enable them to obtain a certified copy of the birth certificate [s.80(3)].

Part 2 is to contain prescribed information about persons who have given notice expressing their wishes, as relatives of adopted persons, as to making contact with those persons [s.80(4)].

The Registrar General may only make an entry in Part 2 of the register for a person who:

- has attained the age of 18 years; and

Adoptions with a foreign element

- the Registrar General is satisfied is a relative of an adopted person and has such information as is necessary to enable them to obtain a certified copy of the record of the adopted person's birth.

Regulations provide for the:

- disclosure of information contained in one Part of the register to persons for whom there is an entry in the other Part; and
- payment of prescribed fees [s.80(6)].

Adoption contact register (supplementary) [s.81]

The Adoption Contact Register is not to be open to public inspection or search [s.81(1)].

In section 80, 'relative', in relation to an adopted person, means any person who (but for their adoption) would be related to them by blood (including half-blood) or marriage [s.81(2)].

The Registrar General must not give any information entered in the register to any person except in accordance with section 80(6)(a) or regulations.

Adoptions with a foreign element

BRINGING CHILDREN INTO AND OUT OF THE UK

Restrictions on bringing children in [s.83]

Section 83 applies where a person habitually resident in the British Islands – a 'British resident' – alone or jointly with another person:

- brings, or causes another to bring, a child habitually resident outside the British Islands to the UK for the purpose of adoption by the British resident; or

- at any time brings, or causes another to bring into the UK, a child adopted by the British resident under an external adoption effected within the previous 12 months [s.83(1)].

Section 83 does not apply if the child is intended to be adopted under a Convention adoption order [s.83(2)].

An 'external' adoption means an adoption, other than a Convention adoption, of a child effected under the law of any country or territory outside the British Islands, whether or not the adoption is:

- an adoption within the meaning of Chapter 4; or
- a full adoption (within the meaning of s.88(3)) [s.83(3)].

For regulations, see the Adoptions with a Foreign Element Regulations 2005.

If a person brings, or causes another to bring, a child into the UK at any time in circumstances where section 83 applies, they are guilty of an offence if, before that time, or before any later time prescribed in the regulations:

- they have not complied with any requirement or conditions imposed by those regulations [s.83(7)].

A person guilty of an offence under section 83 is liable:

- on summary conviction to imprisonment for a term not exceeding six months, or a fine not exceeding the statutory maximum, or both;
- on conviction on indictment, to imprisonment for a term not exceeding 12 months, or a fine, or both [s.83(8)].

Giving parental responsibility prior to adoption abroad [s.84]

The High Court may, on an application by persons who the court is satisfied intend to adopt a child under the law of a country or territory outside the British Islands, make an order giving parental responsibility for the child to them [s.84(1)].

An order under section 84 may not give parental responsibility to persons who the court is satisfied meet those requirements as to domicile, or habitual residence, in England and Wales which have to be met if an adoption order is to be made in favour of those persons [s.84(2)].

An order under section 84 may not be made unless the requirements prescribed by regulation 10 of the Adoptions with a Foreign Element Regulations 2005 are satisfied [s.84 (3)].

An application for an order under section 84 may not be made unless at all times during the preceding ten weeks the child's home was with the applicant or, in the case of an application by two people, both of them [s.84(4)].

Section 46(2) to (4) has effect in relation to an order under section 84 as it has effect in relation to adoption orders [s.84(5)].

Regulation 11 of the Adoptions with a Foreign Element Regulations 2005 provides for any provision of this Act which refers to adoption orders to apply, with or without modifications, to orders under section 84 [s.84(6)].

Restrictions on taking children out of the UK [s.85]

A child who is a Commonwealth citizen, or is habitually resident in the UK, must not be removed from the UK to a place outside the British Islands for the purpose of adoption unless the prospective adopters have parental responsibility for the child by virtue of an order under section 84, or they are removed under the authority of an order under section 49 Adoption (Scotland) Act 1978 [see also ss.59 and 60 of the Adoption and Children (Scotland Act) 2007] and Article 57 Adoption (Northern Ireland) Order 1987 [s.85(1); (2)].

Removing a child from the UK includes arranging to do so, and the circumstances in which a person arranges to remove a child from the UK include those where they:

- enter into an arrangement or initiate or take part in any negotiations for that purpose; or

- cause another person to take any step mentioned in either of the above paragraphs [s.85(3)].

A person who removes a child from the UK in contravention of section 85(1) is guilty of an offence [s.85(4)].

A person is not guilty of an offence under section 85(4) of causing a person to take any step mentioned in the first or second paragraphs of section 85(3) unless it is proved that they knew or had reason to suspect the step taken would contravene section 85(1).

A person guilty of an offence under section 85 is liable:

- on summary conviction to imprisonment for a term not exceeding six months, or a fine not exceeding the statutory maximum, or both;
- on conviction on indictment, to imprisonment for a term not exceeding 12 months, or a fine, or both [s.85(6)].

Power to modify ss.83 & s.85 [s.86]

Regulations under section 86 may provide for section 83 (restrictions on bringing a child into the UK) not to apply if (as well as satisfying specified conditions) adopters/prospective adopters are natural parents, natural relatives or guardians of the child in question or if the British resident in question is a partner of a parent of the child [s.86(1)].

Regulations may also provide for section 85(1) (restriction on taking child out of the UK) to apply with modifications, or not to apply, if (as well as any prescribed conditions being met) the prospective adopters are parents, relatives or guardians of the child in question (or one of them is), or the prospective adopter is a partner of a parent of the child.

No regulations have yet been made under section 86.

OVERSEAS ADOPTIONS

Overseas adoptions [s.87]

In this Act, 'overseas adoption':

Adoptions with a foreign element

- means an adoption of a description specified in an order made by the Secretary of State, being a description of adoptions effected under the law of any country or territory outside the British Islands; but

- does not include a Convention adoption [s.87(1)].

The Adoptions with a Foreign Element Regulations 2005 prescribe requirements that ought to be met by an adoption of any description effected after commencement of the regulations for it to be an overseas adoption for purposes of this Act [s.86 (2)].

Annulment etc of overseas or Hague Convention adoptions [s.89]

Section 89 enables the High Court to:

- annul a Convention adoption or Convention adoption order on the grounds the adoption is contrary to public policy;

- by order provide for an overseas adoption or a determination under section 91 (overseas determinations and orders) to cease to be valid;

- decide the extent, if any, to which a determination under section 91 has been affected by a subsequent determination under that section;

- decide that an overseas adoption or a determination under section 91 is to be treated as invalid (if contrary to public policy or because the authority which purported to authorise it was not competent to do so).

Miscellaneous

RESTRICTIONS

Restriction on arranging adoptions etc [s.92]

A person who is neither an adoption agency nor acting in pursuance of an order of the High Court must **not** take any of the following steps:

- asking a person other than an adoption agency to provide a child for adoption;
- asking a person other than an adoption agency to provide prospective adopters for a child;
- offering to find a child for adoption;
- offering a child for adoption to a person other than an adoption agency;
- handing over a child to any person other than an adoption agency with a view to the child's adoption by that or another person;
- receiving a child handed over to them in contravention of the paragraph immediately above;
- entering into an agreement with any person for the adoption of a child, or for the purpose of facilitating the adoption of a child, where no adoption agency is acting on behalf of the child in the adoption;
- initiating or taking part in negotiations of which the purpose is the conclusion of an agreement within the paragraph immediately above;
- causing another person to take any of the steps mentioned in the preceding eight paragraphs.

If the prospective adopters are parents, relatives or guardians of the child (or one of them is), or the prospective adopter is the partner of a parent of the child, they are **not** prohibited from:

- offering a child for adoption to a person other than an adoption agency;
- handing over a child to any person other than an adoption agency with a view to the child's adoption by that or another person;
- entering into an agreement with any person for the child's adoption or facilitation of adoption, where no agency is acting on behalf of the child;
- initiating or taking part in negotiations in order to conclude the above agreement;
- causing another person to take any of the above steps.

Offence of breaching restrictions under s.92 [s.93]

If a person contravenes section 92(1), they are guilty of an offence and, if that person is an adoption society, the person who manages the society is also guilty of the offence [s.93(1)].

A person is not guilty of receiving a child handed over to them for adoption unless it is proved that they knew or had reason to suspect that this was the case.

A person is not guilty of an offence of causing a person to take any of the prohibited steps of section 91(2) unless it is proved that they knew or had reason to suspect they would be doing so.

A person guilty of an offence under section 93 is liable on summary conviction to imprisonment for a term not exceeding six months, or a fine not exceeding £10,000, or both [s.93(5)].

Restrictions on reports [s.94]

The Restriction on Preparations of Adoption Reports Regulations 2005 make it clear that only a registered and suitably qualified social worker may prepare a report for any person about the suitability of a child for adoption or of a person to adopt a child or about the adoption, or placement for adoption, of a child [s.94(1)].

Miscellaneous

A person is guilty of an offence if they:

- contravene section 94(1); or
- cause a person to prepare a report, or submit to any person a report which has been prepared, in contravention of that subsection [s.94(2)].

The person who manages the society is also guilty of the offence if a person who works for an adoption society:

- contravenes section 94(1); or
- causes a person to prepare a report, or submits to any person a report which has been prepared, in contravention of that subsection [s.94(2)].

A person is not guilty of an offence under section 94(2) (causing a person to prepare a report etc) unless it is proved they knew or had reason to suspect that the report would be, or had been, prepared in contravention of section 94(1) [s.94(4)].

A person guilty of an offence under section 94 is liable on summary conviction to imprisonment for a term not exceeding six months, or a fine not exceeding level 5 on the standard scale, or both [s.94(5)].

Prohibition of certain payments [s.95]

Section 95 applies to any payment (other than an excepted payment) which is made for or in consideration of:

- the adoption of a child;
- giving any consent required in connection with the adoption of a child;
- removing from the UK a child who is a Commonwealth citizen, or is habitually resident in the UK, to a place outside the British Islands for the purpose of adoption;

Miscellaneous

- a person (who is neither an adoption agency nor acting in pursuance of an order of the High Court or family court) taking any step mentioned in section 92(2);

- preparing, causing to be prepared or submitting a report, preparation of which contravenes section 94(1) [s.95(1)].

A person is guilty of an offence (and liable on summary conviction to imprisonment for up to six months, a fine not exceeding £10,000 or both [s.95(4)] if they:

- make any payment to which section 95 applies;

- agree or offer to make any such payment; or

- receive or agree to receive or attempt to obtain any such payment [s.95(3)].

Excepted payments [s.96]

A payment is an 'excepted' one if it is made:

- by virtue of, or in accordance with provisions of this Act, the Adoption (Scotland) Act 1978 [see also the Adoption and Children (Scotland) Act 2007] or the Adoption (Northern Ireland) Order 1987 [s.96(1)];

- to a registered adoption society in respect of expenses reasonably incurred by the society in connection with the adoption/proposed adoption of a child, by a parent or guardian of a child, or person who adopts or proposes to adopt a child [s.96(2)];

- in respect of any legal or medical expenses incurred or to be incurred by any person in connection with an application to a court which they have made/proposes to make for an adoption order, a placement order, or an order under section 26, section 51A or section 84 [s.96(3)];

- for removing from the UK a child who is a Commonwealth citizen or habitually resident in the UK, to a place outside the British Islands for the purpose of adoption so long as the condition in section 85(2) is met (prospective adopters have parental responsibility or authorisation in relevant Scottish or Northern Irish law), and payment is for travel and accommodation expenses reasonably incurred in removing the child from the UK for the purpose of adoption [s.96(4)].

INFORMATION

Pre-commencement adoptions: information [s.98]

The Adoption Information and Intermediary Services (Pre-Commencement Adoptions) Regulations 2005 make provision for the purpose of:

- assisting persons adopted before the appointed day who have attained the age of 18 to obtain information in relation to their adoption;
- facilitating contact between such persons and their relatives [s.98(1)]; and
- facilitating contact between such person's relatives and persons with a prescribed relationship to the adopted person.

For that purpose the regulations may confer functions on:

- registered adoption support agencies;
- the Registrar General;
- adoption agencies [s.98(2)].

Proceedings under the Adoption and Children Act 2002 in the High Court or the Family Court may be heard and determined in private [s.101].

THE CHILDREN AND FAMILY COURT ADVISORY AND SUPPORT SERVICE

Officers of the service [s.102]

Rules (the Family Procedure Rules 2010) must provide for the appointment of an officer of the Children and Family Court Advisory and Support Service ('the Service') (CAFCASS) for the purposes of:

Miscellaneous

- any relevant application;
- signification by any person of any consent to placement or adoption [s.102(1)].

A report prepared in pursuance of the rules on matters relating to the welfare of a child must:

- deal with prescribed matters (unless the court orders otherwise); and
- be made in the manner required by the court [s.102(4)].

A CAFCASS officer must **not** be appointed under section 102 if they:

- are employed by the local authority which made the application (application for the making, varying or revocation of a placement order);
- are employed by the adoption agency which placed the child (application for an adoption order in respect of a child placed for adoption); or
- are within a description prescribed by the above rules [s.102(5)].

Rights of officers of the service to have access to adoption agency records [s.103]

Where a CAFCASS officer has been appointed to act under section 102(1), they have the right at all reasonable times to examine and take copies of any records of, or held by, an adoption agency compiled in connection with the making, or proposed making, by any person of any application under this Part in respect of the child concerned [s.103(1)].

Where the officer takes a copy of any record which they are entitled to examine under section 103, that copy or any part of it is admissible as evidence of any matter referred to in any:

- report they make to the court in the proceedings; or
- evidence which they give [s.103(2)].

EVIDENCE

Evidence of consent [s.104]

If a document signifying any required consent is witnessed in accordance with rules, it is admissible in evidence without further proof of the signature of the person by whom it was executed [s.104(1)].

A document signifying any such witnessed consent is presumed to be valid unless the contrary is proved [s.104(2)].

Avoiding delay [s.109]

In proceedings in which a question may arise as to whether an adoption order or placement order should be made, or any other question with respect to such an order, the court must (in the light of any rules mentioned in section 109(2)):

- draw up a timetable with a view to determining such a question without delay; and
- give such directions as it considers appropriate for the purpose of ensuring that the timetable is adhered to [s.109(1)].

Service of notices etc [s.110]

Any notice or information required to be given by virtue of this Act may be given by post [s.110].

Special guardianship [s.14A–G Children Act 1989 introduced by s.115]

This section summarises what is (for purposes of adoption-related work) the most significant amendment made by the ACA 2002 to the Children Act 1989, i.e. the introduction of 'special guardianship' via section 115.

Purpose of special guardianship order

Special guardianship orders are intended to meet the needs of children who cannot live with their birth parents, for whom adoption is not appropriate but who could still benefit from a legally secure placement.

Definition and conditions for making special guardianship order [s.14A Children Act 1989]

A 'special guardianship order' is an order appointing one or more individuals to be a child's 'special guardian' (or special guardians) [s.14A(1) Children Act 1989].

A special guardian must:

- be aged 18 or over; and
- not be a parent of the child in question [s.14A(2) Children Act 1989].

The court may make a special guardianship order with respect to any child on the application of an individual (or joint application of more than one such individual – who need not be couples or partners) who:

- is/are entitled to make such an application with respect to the child; or
- has/have obtained the leave of the court to make the application [s.14A(3) Children Act 1989].

A person who is, or was at any time within the last six months, a local authority foster carer of a child may not apply for a special guardianship order with respect to that child unless they have the authority's consent, is a relative or the child has lived with them for a total of at least one year preceding the application [effect of s.14A(4) Children Act 1989].

Eligibility to make an application for special guardianship order [s.14A(5)–(7) Children Act 1989 as amended]

The individuals who are entitled to apply for a special guardianship order with respect to a child are:

- any guardian of the child;

Special guardianship

- any individual in whose favour a 'live with' child arrangements order is in force with respect to the child;
- any person with whom the child has lived for at least three years (of the last five years including a period in the three months before the application is made);
- where a 'live with' child arrangements order is in force with respect to the child, any person who has consent of those persons in whose favour the child arrangements order was made;
- where the child is in the care of the local authority, any person who has the consent of that authority;
- any person who has the consent of each of those (if any) who have parental responsibility for the child;
- a local authority foster carer or a relative with whom the child has lived for a period of at least one year immediately preceding the application [s.14A(5) as amended by s.38 C&YPA 2008].

The court may also make a special guardianship order with respect to a child in any family proceedings (adoption proceedings are family proceedings) in which a question arises with respect to the welfare of the child if:

- an application for the order has been made by an individual (or more than one such individual jointly) who is entitled to or has obtained the court's leave to do so;
- the court considers that a special guardianship order should be made even though no such application has been made [s.14A(6) Children Act 1989].

No individual may make an application under section 14A(3) or (6) unless, they have given three months written notice of their intention to make the application:

- if the child in question is being looked after by a local authority, to that local authority, or

Special guardianship

- otherwise, to the local authority in whose area the individual is ordinarily resident [s.14A(7) Children Act 1989].

Response to a notice of intention to apply for special guardianship order [s.14A(8)–(13) Children Act 1989]

On receipt of such a notice, the local authority must investigate the matter and prepare a report for the court [s.14A(8)].

The court may itself ask a local authority to conduct such an investigation and prepare such a report, and the local authority must do so [s.14A(9) Children Act 1989].

The local authority may make such arrangements as it sees fit for any person to act on its behalf in connection with conducting an investigation or preparing a report referred to in section 14A(8) or (9) [s.14A(10) Children Act 1989].

The court may not make a special guardianship order unless it has received a report dealing with the matters referred to in section 14A(8) [s.14A(11) Children Act 1989].

Where a person applies for leave to make an application for a special guardianship order, the court in deciding whether to grant leave must have particular regard to:

- the nature of the proposed application;
- the applicant's connection with the child;
- any risk there might be of that proposed application disrupting the child's life to such an extent that they would be harmed by it; and
- (where they are looked after by a local authority) the authority's plans for the child's future and the wishes and feelings of the child's parents [s.14A(12) Children Act 1989].

When a placement order is in force, no special guardianship order may be made in respect of a child unless an application has been made for an adoption order and the applicant for the guardianship order has obtained the court's leave under section 29(5) or (if they are a guardian of the child) has obtained the court's leave under section 47(5). Where leave has been given, the requirement for three months service of the notice in section 14A(7) applications does not apply [effect of s.14A(13) Children Act 1989].

Making a special guardianship order [s.14B Children Act 1989]

Before making a special guardianship order, the court must consider whether, if the order were made:

- a contact order should also be made with respect to the child; and
- any section 8 order in force with respect to the child should be varied or discharged [s.14B(1) Children Act 1989];
- whether any enforcement order should be revoked or contact activity direction should be discharged.

On making a special guardianship order, the court may also:

- give leave for the child to be known by a new surname;
- grant the leave to remove the child from the UK required by section 14C(3)(b), either generally or for specified purposes [s.14B(2) Children Act 1989].

Effect of a special guardianship order [s.14C Children Act 1989]

The effect of a special guardianship order is that while the order remains in force:

- a special guardian appointed by the order has parental responsibility for the child in respect of whom it is made; and
- subject to any other order in force with respect to the child under the Children Act, is entitled to exercise parental responsibility to the exclusion of any other person with parental responsibility for the child (apart from another special guardian) [s.14C(1) Children Act 1989].

A special guardian is **not** entitled to provide consent to key decisions where statute or case law require the consent of more than one person with parental responsibility in a matter affecting the child, e.g:

Special guardianship

- sterilisation/circumcision;
- adoption or placement for adoption.

While a special guardianship order is in force with respect to a child, no person may (without either the written consent of every person who has parental responsibility for the child or the leave of the court):

- cause the child to be known by a new surname; or
- remove the child from the UK [s.14C(3) Children Act 1989].

The child's special guardian is allowed to remove the child from the UK for a period of less than three months [s.14C(4) Children Act 1989].

If the child with respect to whom a special guardianship order is in force dies, the child's special guardian must take reasonable steps to give notice of that fact to each:

- parent of the child with parental responsibility; and
- guardian of the child.

If the child has more than one special guardian, and one has taken such steps in relation to a particular parent or guardian, any other special guardian need not also do so [s.14C(5) Children Act 1989].

Variation and discharge of a special guardianship order [s.14D Children Act 1989]

The court may vary or discharge a special guardianship order on the application of:

- the special guardian (or any of them, if there are more than one);
- any parent or guardian of the child concerned;
- any individual in whose favour a live with child arrangements order is in force with respect to the child;
- any individual not falling into the above categories, who has, or immediately before the making of the special guardianship order had, parental responsibility for the child;

Special guardianship

- the child themself; or
- a local authority designated in a care order with respect to the child [s.14D(1) Children Act 1989].

In any family proceedings in which a question arises with respect to the welfare of a child with respect to whom a special guardianship order is in force, the court may also vary or discharge the special guardianship order if it considers that the order should be varied or discharged, even though no application has been made under section 14D(1) [s.14D(2) Children Act 1989].

The following must obtain the leave of the court before making an application under section 14D(1):

- the child;
- any parent or guardian of the child;
- any step-parent who has acquired, and has not lost, parental responsibility for the child by virtue of section 4A;
- any individual (other than a special guardian, parent or guardian in whose favour a live with child arrangements order is in force) who immediately before the making of the special guardianship order had, but no longer has, parental responsibility for the child.

Where the person applying for leave to make an application under section 14D(1) is the child, the court may only grant leave if it is satisfied that the child has sufficient understanding to make the proposed application [s.14D(4) Children Act 1989].

The court may not grant leave to a person (other than the child or the special guardian) under section 14D(3) unless it is satisfied that there has been a significant change in circumstances since the making of the special guardianship order [s.14D(5) Children Act 1989].

Special guardianship order: supplementary provisions [s.14E Children Act 1989]

In proceedings in which any question of making, varying or discharging a special guardianship order arises, the court shall (in the light of any rules made by virtue of section 14E(3)):

- draw up a timetable with a view to determining the question without delay; and
- give such directions as it considers appropriate for the purpose of ensuring, so far as is reasonably practicable, that the timetable is adhered to [s.14E(1) Children Act 1998].

Section 14E(1) applies also in relation to proceedings in which any other question with respect to a special guardianship order arises. A special guardianship order, or an order varying one, may contain provisions which are to have effect for a specified period [s.14E(4) Children Act 1989].

Special guardianship order support services [s.14F Children Act 1989]

Each local authority must make arrangements for the provision within their area of special guardianship support services, i.e:

- counselling, advice and information; and
- such other services as are prescribed [s.14F(1) Children Act 1989].

At the request of any of the following persons, a local authority may carry out an assessment of that person's needs for special guardianship support services:

- a child with respect to whom a special guardianship order is in force;
- a special guardian;
- a parent.

Special guardianship

A local authority must carry out an assessment if the relevant child is, or was immediately before the order was made, a looked after child [Reg.11 of the Special Guardianship Regulations 2005].

A local authority may, at the request of any other person, carry out an assessment of that person's needs for special guardianship support services [s.14F(4) Children Act 1989].

Where, as a result of an assessment, a local authority decides that a person has needs for special guardianship support services, it must then decide whether to provide any such services to that person [s.14F(5) Children Act 1989].

The local authority must prepare a plan in accordance with which special guardianship support services are to be provided to the person and keep the plan under review, **if**:

- the local authority decides to provide any special guardianship support services to a person; and
- the circumstances fall within a prescribed description [s.14F(6) Children Act 1989].

A local authority may provide special guardianship support services (or any part of them) by securing their provision by:

- another local authority; or
- a person as defined in the Special Guardianship Regulations 2005.

A local authority may also arrange with any such authority or person for that other authority or that person to carry out the local authority's functions in relation to assessments under section 14.

A local authority may carry out an assessment of the needs of any person for the purposes of special guardianship at the same time as an assessment of their needs is made under any other provision of the Children Act or under any other enactment [s.14F(10) Children Act 1989].

Section 27 Children Act 1989 (co-operation between authorities) applies in relation to the exercise of functions of a local authority introduced by section 115 as it applies in relation to the exercise of functions of a local authority under Part 3 [s.14F(11) Children Act 1989].

Special guardianship order support services: representations [s.14G Children Act 1989]

Every local authority shall establish a procedure for considering representations (including complaints) made to it by any person to whom it may provide special guardianship support services about the discharge of its functions under section 14 in relation to them [s.14G(1) Children Act 1989].

Regulations may be made by the Secretary of State imposing time limits on the making of the above representations [s.14G(2) Children Act 1989].

Advertisements and Adoption and Children Act Register

This section summarises provisions relating to:

- advertisements in the UK;
- the Adoption and Children Act Register;
- other miscellaneous provisions.

ADVERTISEMENTS IN THE UK

Restriction on advertisements etc [s.123]

A person must not publish or distribute an advertisement or information or cause such an advertisement or information to be published or distributed indicating that:

- the parent or guardian of a child wants the child to be adopted;

- a person wants to adopt a child;
- a person other than an adoption agency is willing to make any of the arrangements specified in section 92(2);
- a person other than an adoption agency is willing to receive a child handed over to them with a view to the child's adoption by them or another; or
- a person is willing to remove a child from the UK for the purposes of adoption.

Section 123 applies to information about how to do anything which would constitute an offence under the Adoption (Scotland) Act 1978, the Adoption (Northern Ireland) Order 1987 (whether or not the information includes a warning that doing the thing in question may constitute an offence) or information about a particular child as a child available for adoption.

Publishing or distributing an advertisement or information means publishing it or distributing it to the public and includes doing so by electronic means (for example, by means of the internet), and the public includes selected members of the public as well as the public generally or any section of the public.

Section 123(1) does not apply to publication or distribution by or on behalf of an adoption agency [s.123(5)].

References to an adoption agency in section 123 include a prescribed person outside the UK exercising functions corresponding to those of an adoption agency, if the functions are being exercised in prescribed circumstances.

In this section 'adoption agency' includes a Scottish or Northern Irish adoption agency, references to adoption are to the adoption of persons, wherever they may be habitually resident, effected under the law of any country or territory, whether within or outside the British Islands [s.123(9)].

Advertisements and Adoption and Children Act Register

Offence of breaching restriction under s.123 [s.124]

A person who contravenes section 123(1) is guilty of an offence [s.124(1)] but a person is not guilty of an offence under section 124 unless it is proved they knew or had reason to suspect that section 123 applied to the advertisement or information [s.124(2)].

A person guilty of an offence under section 124 is liable on summary conviction to imprisonment for a term not exceeding three months, or a fine not exceeding level 5 on the standard scale, or both [s.124(3)].

ADOPTION AND CHILDREN ACT REGISTER

Adoption and Children Act Register [s.125]

The Secretary of State may establish and maintain a register, to be called the Adoption and Children Act Register, containing:

- prescribed information about children who are suitable for adoption, children for whom a local authority in England are considering adoption, and prospective adopters who are suitable to adopt a child;

- prescribed information about persons included in the register in pursuance of the above paragraph, in respect of things occurring after their inclusion [s.125(1)].

Information to be contained in the register may be in any form the Secretary of State considers appropriate [s.125(5)].

Note: Section 125 came into force on 27.07.14. Amendments introduced by the Children and Families Act 2014 included extending the register to cover Welsh, Scottish and Northern Irish adoption agencies and their children and prospective adopters [s.125(1A)].

The Adoption and Children Act Register was operated by BAAF, and latterly by Coram, until it was closed by the Secretary of State in 2019. There are currently no plans to reintroduce a Register in England.

Annex A of the Guidance contains a summary of offences under the Act and the time limits for bringing proceedings.

PART II
REGULATIONS

Fostering for Adoption

Regulation 25A of the Care Planning, Placement and Case Review (England) Regulations 2010 which came into force on 1 July 2013 provides for an approved prospective adopter (by any adoption agency) to be temporarily approved by a child's local authority as a foster carer for that child, without having to go through the full foster carer assessment and approval process. (If the person has already been approved as a foster carer under the Fostering Services Regulations, by any fostering agency, there is no need to approve them again for a named child, under the CPPR 2010 Regulations.) Regulation 25A does not apply if:

- the adopter does not wish to foster the child prior to the placement order being made;
- a prospective carer wishes to be approved as a foster carer but not also as an adopter.

Under regulation 25A(1) and (2), the child's local authority can only temporarily approve a prospective adopter as a foster carer for that child if it:

- is satisfied that it is the most appropriate placement for the child, and it is in the child's best interests to be placed with them;
- has assessed the carer's suitability to care for the child as a foster carer;
- considers that placing the child with that carer will safeguard and promote the child's welfare and meet the child's needs as set out in the care plan.

The temporary approval as a foster carer will be terminated if:

- the child's placement with the prospective adopter is terminated;
- the prospective adopter's approval as an adopter is terminated;

- the prospective adopter is fully approved as a foster carer;
- the prospective adopter no longer wishes to be temporarily approved as a foster carer;
- the child is placed for adoption with the approved prospective adopter [CPPR 2010 reg.25A(3)].

See also Statutory Guidance on Fostering for Adoption in Children Act 1989 Guidance & Regulations Volume 2: Care Planning, Placement & Case Review.

Regulations

The following part provides a summary of regulations issued under the Act.

The Adoption Agencies Regulations 2005

These regulations (as amended by the Adoption Agencies and Independent Review of Determinations (Amendment) Regulations 2011 and the Adoption Agencies (Miscellaneous Amendments) Regulations 2013) apply in England only and govern the operation of adoption agencies.

PANEL

Although there is no requirement to consider permanent fostering plans or matches, a joint adoption and permanence panel can help reduce delay for children by avoiding consideration by separate panels. However, such a panel must comply with these regulations and the Fostering Services Regulations 2011 [Guidance 1.22–24].

Agencies, except those acting as intermediaries only [reg.5], must maintain a central list of suitable panel members, including:

- one or more social workers with three years' relevant post-qualifying experience;
- the agency medical adviser [reg.3(1)].

There is no limit to the number of people on the list, but panels must not be so large that they are unmanageable or intimidating to prospective adopters attending. Relevant experience means in child care social work, including direct adoption work; social workers without such experience may be appointed in addition [Guidance 1.29].

A person on the list can resign, or be removed by the agency if considered no longer suitable, after one month's written notice [reg.3(2)–(3)].

Agencies are expected to discuss any performance shortfall with members and allow time for improvement before terminating membership. For joint panels, all local authorities must agree on termination [Guidance 1.36].

Agencies must have at least one adoption panel with members drawn from the central list to include:

- an independent Chair with the necessary skills and experience;
- one or two vice-chairs [reg.4(1)].

Independent means not a trustee or employee (voluntary agency), member or employee involved in child protection or placement (local authority agency) or an adopter approved by the agency or with a child placed by the agency, unless it is more than 12 months since the adoption order [reg.7].

The panel must have enough members and they must between them have the necessary experience and expertise [reg.4(2)].

Agencies should manage the turnover of members so as to avoid a large number of departures in any one year.

Local authorities may pay reasonable fees to panel members [reg.4(4)].

Two or more local authorities may appoint a joint panel and must agree on the membership [reg.4(3)].

While there is no provision for joint panels between voluntary agencies, more than one branch of the same agency may share a panel [Guidance 1.34].

The quorum for panel meetings is five (six for a joint panel) including the Chair or vice-chair, one social worker with relevant experience; one person present must be an independent member [reg.6(1)].

Panels should meet sufficiently frequently (including at short notice) to enable agencies to dovetail planning for children with court timescales and minimise delay [Guidance 1.25].

Where the panel cannot agree, the Chair has the casting vote [Guidance 1.48].

The panel must take minutes of meetings, including recommendations and reasons [reg.6(2)].

Minutes must not be taken by a panel member [Guidance 1.44].

Agencies must have agency and panel policies and procedures, drawn up in consultation with appropriate people on the central list (and the medical adviser in respect of disclosure of information), and kept under review and revised as necessary [reg.7].

Staff should also have the opportunity to contribute to policy and procedures [Guidance 1.2].

Agencies must appoint a senior member of staff as agency panel adviser (by agreement if a joint panel), who must be a social worker with five years' post-qualifying experience and relevant management experience, to:

- help with maintaining the central list and panels;
- be responsible for training, induction and performance monitoring of those on the central list and panel members and panel administration;

- liaise between agency and panel and give advice to the panel [reg.8].

There should be at least one agency adviser (and a deputy as necessary) with adoption team leader experience or more senior management experience with adoption experience. The adviser is not a panel member and cannot take part in decision-making [Guidance 1.30–31].

The panel adviser should also quality assure reports to the panel in liaison with agency managers, and provide updates to the panel on cases previously presented, especially where the panel recommendation was not accepted [Guidance 1.32–33].

Regulation 8(3) and (4) also requires agencies to appoint at least one registered medical practitioner as agency medical adviser and to consult them on dealing with medical information under the regulations.

Members should be given performance targets and reviewed against these every year. The Chair's performance is to be reviewed by the agency's decision-maker, and feedback on the Chair's performance should be sought from other members and those attending panel [Guidance 1.35].

CONSIDERING ADOPTION FOR A CHILD

Regulations 12–17 cover agency duties when considering adoption for a child.

Agencies must first create a 'child's case record' containing the prescribed information, including the 'child's permanence report' [reg.12(1)].

Statutory timescales for planning must be met or the reasons for not doing so recorded, and agencies must report their performance against timescales to executive bodies six monthly [Guidance 2.2–4].

If reasonably practicable (unless satisfied it has been done by another agency), the agency must:

- counsel the child;

- explain and provide information in writing about the process and legal implications of adoption, in an age-appropriate way;
- ascertain the child's wishes and feelings about adoption, placement, religion and culture, and contact with parents/guardians, relatives and relevant others [reg.13].

Guidance 2.22–26 covers counselling and informing children.

If reasonably practicable (unless satisfied it has been done by another agency), the agency must:

- counsel the child's parent or guardian;
- explain and provide written information to them about adoption and placement procedures; the legal implications of giving consent to placement or future adoption, placement orders, and adoption;
- ascertain the wishes and feelings of the child's parent/guardian and any relevant others about the child, adoption and placement for adoption, religion and culture and contact [reg.14(1) & (2)].

Detailed guidance is given on working with birth fathers and extended families, including case law relating to parents wishing to withhold information from other family members [2.27–47].

If the agency knows the identity of a father without parental responsibility, it must, if appropriate (unless satisfied it has been done by another agency):

- counsel him;
- explain and provide written information about adoption and placement procedures and the legal implications of adoption;
- ascertain his wishes and feelings about the child, adoption and placement for adoption, religion and culture and contact [reg.14(3) & (4)(a)].

As far as possible, the agency must also ascertain if a known father without parental responsibility wishes to acquire it, or to apply for a contact order [reg.14(4)(b)].

Adoption Agencies Regulations

Regulation 15(1) requires agencies to collect as far as possible the information about a child specified in Schedule 1 Part 1.

Unless a child capable of making an informed decision refuses, the agency must arrange a medical examination and obtain a 'child's health report' covering:

- the child's state of health;
- any treatment they are receiving or health care needed; and
- the information specified in Schedule 1 Part 2 [reg.15(2), (3) & (4)].

A medical examination may not be necessary if the medical adviser is satisfied with the information available from recent reports [Guidance 2.54].

As far as is reasonably practicable, agencies must obtain:

- information about the child's family specified in Schedule 1 Part 3; and
- information about the health of the child's parents and siblings specified in Schedule 1 Part 4 [reg.16].

Agencies must prepare a 'child's permanence report' containing:

- information specified in Schedule 1 Parts 1 and 3 (child and family);
- the medical adviser's health summary;
- the child's wishes and feelings [reg.13(1)(c)];
- wishes and feelings of parents/guardians, father without parental responsibility (if consulted under regulation 14) and any relevant others [reg.14(1)(c)];
- the agency's views and proposals as to contact;
- a developmental assessment and any needs arising;
- an assessment of the parenting capacity of parents, guardians or father without parental responsibility (if consulted under regulation 14);

- chronology of agency decisions and actions;
- care options considered and reason for adoption recommendation;
- any other relevant information [reg.17(1)].

Parents (and the child if old enough) should see part or all of the report and any views they express should be included in the report [Guidance 2.65].

Regulation 17 prescribes the reports that are to be taken into account when a local authority is considering whether a child should be placed for adoption:

- child's permanence report;
- health report and any other reports referred to in regulation 15;
- information on the health of each of the child's parents.

The reports must be sent to the panel in cases where the child is relinquished for adoption or where the child is subject to a care order and the parents consent to the child's adoption [Guidance 2.69].

In all other cases, a local authority is prohibited from sending the reports to its adoption panel, and must send them direct to the agency decision-maker.

These amendments seek to reduce delay by eliminating the involvement of its adoption panel in cases where the local authority would be obliged to apply for a placement order.

In cases which have been considered by the panel, the agency decision must take account of the panel's recommendation and no panel member/person on the central list may take part in it.

Guidance sets out the matters to be considered by the agency decision which must be within seven days of receipt of the papers, or of the panel and be based on the final minutes, as applicable [1.56].

If the agency decision-maker is minded not to agree the panel's recommendation, they should discuss this with the agency adviser or medical adviser as appropriate [Guidance 1.55].

If their whereabouts are known, the agency must notify in writing the child's parents or guardians and father without parental responsibility (if consulted under regulation 14) [reg.19(3)].

New regulation 19A requires an agency which has decided that a child should be placed for adoption and has not identified prospective adopters to refer the child to the adoption register as soon as possible, and not later than three months after the agency's decision, and to notify any changes as soon as practicable.

Regulation 20 requires agencies to request the appointment of a CAFCASS officer or, in Wales, a family proceedings officer to witness consent to placement or future adoption under sections 19 or 20 of the Act, and to send the information specified in Schedule 2.

Any notice on file under section 20(4) (not wishing to be informed of adoption application or withdrawing such) must be sent to the court when the agency is notified of an adoption application [reg.12(2)].

Advice on the procedure to be followed in cases where a relinquished child is under six weeks old is found in Guidance 2.48–52.

APPROVING ADOPTERS

Note: See section below on fast-track for foster carers and previous adopters for modifications to the assessment process for these applicants.

Stage 1: Pre-assessment (introduced by regulations 22–30 and Schedule 4 of the Adoption Agencies (Miscellaneous Amendments) Regulations 2013)

Stage 1 applies when an adoption agency has notified a prospective adopter that it has decided to proceed with their pre-assessment.

The adoption agency, in consultation with the prospective adopter, must prepare a Stage 1 plan, to include:

- information about counselling, information and preparation for adoption to be provided under regulation 24;
- procedures for carrying out police checks under regulation 25;

Adoption Agencies Regulations

- details of any training that the prospective adopter has agreed to undertake;
- information about the role of the prospective adopter in the Stage 1 process;
- any applicable timescales;
- information about the process for making a representation (including a complaint) under the 1989 regulations; and
- any other information that the agency considers relevant [reg.23].

Agencies considering prospective adopters must:

- provide any available information and training material;
- counsel them; and
- explain and provide written information about the procedures for and legal implications of adoption and placement for adoption (with specific reference to the proposed country in an intercountry adoption case) [reg.24].

Statutory timescales for recruiting adopters must be met or the reasons for not doing so recorded, and agencies must report their performance against timescales to executive bodies six monthly [Guidance 3.97].

Within five working days of receipt of a completed Registration of Interest form, the agency must decide whether to accept this and must set up a case record ('the prospective adopter's case record') containing:

- the prospective adopter Stage 1 plan;
- the application;
- the prospective adopter assessment plan;
- information and reports obtained under Stage 1;
- the prospective adopter's report and their comments on it;
- panel minutes, including recommendation, reasons and any advice;

Adoption Agencies Regulations

- the agency decision;
- any independent review panel recommendation;
- any prospective adopter's review report and their comments on it;
- the prospective adopter matching plan; and
- any other relevant documents or information [reg. 23(1)].

Agencies may ask prospective adopters for any other reasonable information in writing [reg.23(2)].

Agencies must seek enhanced Disclosure and Barring Service (DBS) certificates for prospective adopters and members of their household aged 18 or over [reg.23(1)].

Agencies may not consider as a prospective adopter anyone where they or a member of the household aged 18 or over has been convicted of or cautioned for any offence listed in regulation 25(3) and Schedule 3 Part 1 [reg.25(2)].

Agencies are also precluded from considering as a prospective adopter anyone where they or a member of the household aged 18 or over has been convicted of or cautioned for any of the repealed offences listed in Schedule 3 Part 2 [reg.25(4)].

Agencies must notify the prospective adopter that they cannot be considered as soon as the agency learns that the prospective adopter or a member of the household is covered by the provisions of regulations 25(2) or (4) [reg.25(5)].

Only the person to whom the conviction relates can be told of the reason for unsuitability [Guidance 3.31–2].

Agencies must arrange preparation for prospective adopters, to cover children available for adoption, the significance of adoption for children and families, contact, the skills adopters need, adoption and placement procedures [reg.24(2)].

Adoption Agencies Regulations

Preparation should be tailored to prospective adopters' circumstances and may be provided in conjunction with neighbouring agencies [Guidance 3.40–41].

The agency must obtain the following information:

- information specified in Schedule 4 Part 1;
- written medical report after full examination, including the information specified in Schedule 4 Part 2 (unless the medical adviser confirms as unnecessary);
- referee interview reports;
- where the adoption agency considers it necessary, obtain a personal reference from the prospective adopter's former spouse, civil partner or partner;
- written report of any relevant information from the prospective adopter's local authority [reg. 26].

The agency must within two months of beginning Stage 1, and taking account of information obtained, decide either to proceed with an assessment or that the prospective adopter is not suitable to adopt a child [reg.27(1) & (2)].

The adoption agency may delay its decision where there are good reasons or at the prospective adopter's request [reg.27(3)].

The adoption agency must notify the prospective adopter in writing as soon as practicable:

- of a decision that they are is not suitable, giving reasons; or
- that the prospective adopter has six months in which to inform the agency that they wish to begin an assessment [reg.27(4) & (5)].

If the prospective adopter notifies the agency that they wish to continue with the assessment more than six months after the agency notice under regulation 27(4), the agency must inform the prospective adopter in writing that it cannot proceed with the assessment process [reg.28(2)].

Stage 2: Assessment (introduced by regulations 22–30 and Schedule 4 of the Adoption Agencies (Miscellaneous Amendments) Regulations 2013)

Stage 2 begins when an adoption agency is contacted by an adopter wishing to proceed with assessment in accordance with regulation 27(4)(b).

The agency, in consultation with the prospective adopter, must prepare a written 'prospective adopter assessment plan' to include the assessment procedure and any timescales, additional counselling or preparation, agreed training, adopter's role, the IRM process and any other relevant information [reg.29].

Guidance now indicates that agencies should discuss with prospective adopters whether they might be interested in a fostering for adoption placement, and include this in the prospective adopter's report [Guidance 3.55–6].

Agencies must prepare a 'prospective adopter's report' including:

- Parts 1 and 3 of Schedule 4;
- medical adviser's health summary;
- any local authority information;
- any observations on counselling, DBS checks and preparation;
- the agency's assessment of suitability to adopt;
- any other relevant information [reg.30(2)].

In an intercountry adoption case, the following additional information is required:

- the proposed 'country of origin';
- confirmation that the prospective adopter is eligible to adopt from that country;
- any additional information required by that country;

- the agency's assessment of the prospective adopter's suitability to adopt a child from overseas [reg.30(3)].

A 'second opinion' report by a manager or social worker should be arranged if there are concerns or issues needing clarification [Guidance 3.57].

Where agencies receive information suggesting that a prospective adopter is unsuitable, they may prepare the prospective adopter's report based on the information collected up to that point ("brief report") [reg.30(4)].

The agency must send the prospective adopter notice of the panel and a copy of the report inviting comments on it within five working days [reg.30(5)].

After five working days or when comments are received, if earlier, the agency must send to the panel:

- the prospective adopter's report and their comments on it;
- the medical report, referee interview reports and any local authority information; and
- any other relevant information [reg.30(6)].

As far as is reasonably practicable, the agency must also send any other information requested by the panel [reg.30(7)].

The panel must consider all prospective adopters referred by the agency and recommend whether the prospective adopter is suitable to adopt a child [reg.30A(1)].

The panel must consider the reports and information sent by the agency, and may take legal advice and ask for any other necessary information [reg.30A(2)].

In relation to a brief report, the panel must either ask the agency to complete a full prospective adopter's report, or recommend that the prospective adopter is unsuitable [reg.30A(3)].

If the panel recommends a prospective adopter as suitable, it may also consider and advise on the number, age, sex and likely needs of children they should adopt [reg.30A(4)].

Prospective adopters must be invited to attend the panel [reg.30A(5)].

Applicants are not obliged to attend and the panel is not to consider failure to attend an indication of unsuitability [Guidance 3.70].

The agency must make a decision as to the prospective adopter's suitability to adopt a child within four months of starting Stage 2 (unless there are exceptional circumstances or the prospective adopter so requests) and, if considered suitable, notify them in writing. Panel members are excluded from taking part in the decision [reg.30B(1)–(4)].

If the agency considers the prospective adopter unsuitable, it must:

- notify them in writing with reasons and the panel's recommendation, if different;
- advise them of the right within 40 working days of the notice to make representations to the agency or apply to the Secretary of State for an independent review [reg.30B(5)].

Where the agency decision-maker does not propose to approve a prospective adopter, the prescribed letter must be used [Guidance 1.57 & 3.80].

If the prospective adopter does not make representations or apply for an IRM review within 40 days, the agency should then make its decision and notify the prospective adopter in writing, with reasons [reg.30B(6)].

If the prospective adopter does make representations, the agency may refer the case back to the panel [reg.30B(7)].

If the agency does refer the case back, the panel must consider it and make a fresh recommendation, and the agency must make a decision based on both the original and the fresh recommendations [reg.30B(8) & (9)(a)].

If the prospective adopter applies for an independent review, the agency must:

- send within 10 days of receiving notice from the Secretary of State all the reports and information sent to the adoption panel, any relevant later information, and the notice with reasons (and panel recommendation if different) [reg.30C];
- make a decision after taking account of the IRM panel recommendation and the original panel recommendation [reg.30B(9)(b)].

The agency must notify the prospective adopter in writing as soon as possible after making its decision, and:

- if the decision is not to approve, give reasons and the panel's recommendation, where different [reg.30B(10)];
- if there was an IRM panel, send a copy of the notice to the Secretary of State [reg.30B(11)].

Fast-track for foster carers and previous adopters

Regulation 30F and Schedule 4A introduce a new fast-track assessment and approval process for foster carers and previous adopters (including intercountry adopters). The requirements are modified for these applicants so that:

- there is no two-stage process, pre-assessment decision or collection of information specified in Schedule 4 Part 3 [reg.22, 27–28 & 30(1)];
- there is no brief report option [reg.30(3) & (4)];
- counselling, information and preparation are provided only if considered necessary [reg.24];
- medicals, police and local authority checks and references are taken up only if considered necessary [regs.25 & 26];
- the prospective adopter's report only includes the agency's observations on medicals, police and local authority checks and references where applicable; and the references and medicals are only sent to the panel where applicable [reg.30(2) & 6(b)];

- the timescale for completing the assessment is four months from the Registration of Interest to the agency decision [reg.30B(1)].

REVIEWS OF APPROVED ADOPTERS

Agencies are required to review approved adopters unless a child has been placed or the agency is considering placing a child under regulations 31–33, or, in an intercountry case, the adopter has been linked with and visited a child overseas [reg.30D(1)].

Agencies must carry out reviews at least annually, and must:

- collect any information necessary to review the prospective adopter's suitability to adopt;
- take account of the prospective adopter's views [reg.30D(2) & (3)].

If, on reviewing the case, the agency considers the prospective adopter no longer suitable, it must:

- prepare a 'prospective adopter's review report' with reasons;
- send the prospective adopter notice of the panel and a copy of the report inviting comments on it within 10 working days [reg.30D(4)].

After 10 working days or when comments are received, if earlier, the agency must send to the panel:

- the prospective adopter's review report and their comments on it; and
- as far as is reasonably practicable, any other information requested by the panel [reg.30D(5) & (6)].

The panel must consider the prospective adopter's review report and comments on it, any other information, and recommend whether the prospective adopter remains suitable to adopt a child [reg.30D(7)].

The agency must make a decision as to continuing suitability, and the requirements of regulation 30B(2) to (11) apply to this decision as to the original decision [reg.30D(8)].

INTERCOUNTRY ADOPTERS

If approving a prospective adopter in intercountry cases, the agency must send the following to the Secretary of State:

- its decision and any recommendations as to the age, sex and likely needs of a child they may be suitable for;
- any reports and information sent to the panel;
- the panel minutes including recommendation and reasons;
- any IRM panel minutes including recommendation and reasons; and
- any other relevant information [reg.30E].

See Annex C of the 2005 Guidance for further information on the procedure in adoptions with a foreign element (under revision at time of publication).

Agencies must refer domestic adopters to the Adoption Register as soon as possible (and no later than three months) after approval if they have not identified a child as a potential match, provided the adopter consents [reg.30G].

MATCHING A CHILD WITH APPROVED ADOPTERS

Statutory timescales for matching must be met or the reasons for not doing so recorded [Guidance 4.1–2].

Matches must not be delayed because prospective adopters do not share the child's ethnic origin if they can meet the child's other needs [Guidance 4.4–8].

Agencies must prepare a matching plan in consultation with the adopter, to include information about:

- the agency's duties in relation to matching and placement;
- the adopter's role in identifying a child;
- how to make a complaint or representation; and
- any other matter considered relevant [reg.30H].

When considering a 'proposed placement', agencies must meet the prospective adopters, counsel them and give them information (including the child's permanence report) and seek their views on the proposed placement and any contact arrangements [reg.31(1)].

Agencies must provide prospective adopters with full information about the child and their background [Guidance 4.23–5].

If proposing to proceed with the placement:

- local authority agencies must assess the child and adoptive family for support needs;
- voluntary agencies must advise the adopters that they can approach the local authority for an assessment and, if they ask, pass on reports.

All agencies must consider contact arrangements, and prepare an 'adoption placement report' containing the prescribed information [reg.31(2)].

The agency must give prospective adopters a copy of the report and 10 working days to comment on it, after which it will be sent to the panel (with any comments received) together with the child's permanence report and the prospective adopter's report [reg.31(3) & (4)].

In an inter-agency case, the other agency must be consulted before the proposed placement is referred to the panel, and a child's or adopter's file (as the case may be) must be opened [reg.31(6)–(8)].

Agencies must not allow inter-agency fees to prevent placement of a child [Guidance 4.19].

The panel must consider any proposed placement referred by the agency and (having regard to s.1(2), (4) & (5) of the Act) recommend whether the child should be placed with the prospective adopter [reg.32(1) & (2)].

Panels can consider approval and match at the same meeting to avoid delay in appropriate cases [Guidance 4.33].

The panel must consider the reports sent by the agency, and may take legal advice and ask for more information [reg.32(2)(a)–(c)].

The panel must also consider – and if approving the placement, may advise on – proposed support arrangements (local authorities), contact and any necessary restrictions on the exercise of parental responsibility [reg.32(3) & (4)].

A detailed discussion of the considerations in relation to sharing and restricting parental responsibility is contained in the Adoption Guidance Ch.5.16–23.

The agency must make a decision (panel members taking no part) as to the proposed placement based on the panel recommendation, and as soon as possible notify in writing:

- the adopter/s;
- if their whereabouts are known, the parent/guardian and if appropriate, a father without parental responsibility (if consulted under regulation 14) [reg.33(1)–(3)].

If the agency decides the placement should proceed, it must explain this to the child in an age-appropriate way [reg.33(4)].

Agencies must place on the child's file:

- the prospective adopter's report;
- the adoption placement report and the adopters' comments on it;
- panel minutes with recommendations, reasons and any advice;
- decisions and notices under this regulation [reg.33(5)].

In intercountry cases, agencies must send the adopters any information from overseas about a child to be placed (unless they have a copy already), consider and discuss it with the adopters, and if necessary counsel them and supply any further information [reg.34].

If an agency has decided to place a child with adopters and met them to discuss arrangements, it must send them as soon as possible an 'adoption placement plan' covering the matters specified in Schedule 5 [reg.35(1) & (2)].

A draft of the placement plan should form the basis for a placement planning meeting with the adopters and others [Guidance Ch.5.3].

The child may be placed once the adopters have agreed to the placement provided that:

- the agency is authorised to place the child; or
- the child is under six weeks and either the parent/guardian has consented to placement or there is a placement order [reg.35(3) & (4)].

A placement should not proceed when a local authority is aware of a parent's application for leave to challenge a placement order [Guidance 5.2].

If the child is already in placement, the agency must write to the adopter with the date of placement for adoption [reg.35(5)].

Agencies must, before placement for adoption:

- notify the adopter's GP and send health information about the child;
- notify the local authority (if different) and the local health body; and
- for a school age child, notify the education authority and send education information [reg.35(6)].

Agencies must notify prospective adopters of any change in placement plan [reg.35(7)].

Agencies must place on the child's file:

- consent to placement where there is no placement order for a child under six weeks; and
- the placement plan and any changes to it [reg.35(8)].

Adoption Agencies Regulations

REVIEWS OF CHILDREN IN ADOPTION CASES

Agencies authorised to place a child for adoption who is not yet placed must review the case after three months and then every six months until placement [reg.36(1)].

Where a child is placed for adoption, agencies must:

- review the case within four weeks; three months after the first review; and then every six months until the child moves or is adopted; and
- visit the child and adopter/s weekly until the first review and as necessary thereafter, and write a report of each visit; and
- advise and assist the adopter/s as necessary [reg.36(2), (3) & (4)].

Visits should be shared between the child's and the adopter's social workers. Placing agencies may make arrangements with another local authority to visit a child placed out of the area. Children should be seen alone unless old enough to refuse [Guidance Ch.5.24–30].

As far as is reasonably practicable, agencies must seek the views of the child, the adopters and any other relevant person for each review [reg.36(5)].

Agencies must ensure that reviews cover:

- the continued appropriateness of placement;
- the child's needs, welfare and development, and any necessary changes;
- contact arrangements;
- arrangements for exercise of parental responsibility;
- adoption support services;
- health and education in consultation with the relevant bodies;
- review frequency (subject to regulation 36(1) & (3)) [reg.36(5) & (6)].

If a child on a placement order has not been placed for adoption by the six months review, the agency must find out why, and consider whether any action is needed and if it is still appropriate to place the child [reg.36(7)].

As far as is reasonably practicable, after a review agencies must notify the child (if old enough), the adopters and any other relevant person of the outcome [reg.36(8)].

Agencies must record on the child's file all information obtained for a review, including the child's views, the record of any meeting and of any decisions made [reg.36(9)].

Regulation 36(10) requires agencies to carry out a review of a child returned by the adopters between 28 and 42 days after the disruption, and consider:

- the continued appropriateness of placement;
- the child's needs, welfare and development, and any necessary changes;
- contact arrangements; and
- health and education in consultation with the relevant bodies.

If a placement disrupts, responsibility for the child rests with the placing authority (before adoption) or the adopters' area authority (after adoption) [Guidance 5.31–2].

Regulation 37 requires local authorities and voluntary agencies which accommodate children to appoint as an independent reviewing officer a registered social worker with sufficient experience, where 'independent' means, if an agency employee, not involved in the case or its management in any way [reg.37(1)–(4)].

Reviewing officers must, as far as is reasonably practicable, chair all review meetings, and ensure the requirements of regulation 36 are met, and in particular:

- the child's views are taken into account;

- people are identified to carry out decisions; and
- any failure to review or implement review decisions is reported to a senior officer [reg.37(5) & (6)].

Reviewing officers must assist a child who wishes to bring court proceedings to obtain legal advice or identify an appropriate adult to assist or act on the child's behalf [reg.37(7)].

Agencies must notify the independent reviewing officer (IRO) of any change in circumstances or any failure to implement review decisions [reg.37(8)].

Regulation 38 provides for what happens if a parent withdraws consent given under section 19 or 20 of the Act [reg.38(1)]. In this event:

- voluntary agencies must immediately consider whether to inform the local authority where the child is [reg.38(3)];
- local authorities must immediately review the decision to place for adoption, and, if they decide to apply for a placement order, notify as soon as possible the parent or guardian, a father without parental responsibility (if consulted under regulation 14) and the adopters if the child is already placed [reg.38(2)].

RECORDS

Agencies must ensure that children's and adopters' records are kept securely and confidentially, and are protected from theft, unauthorised disclosure, damage or destruction, for as long as necessary [regs.39–41].

Agencies must have systems in place to protect electronically stored records [Guidance 6.5–6].

Agencies must allow access to records and disclose information as required and must record any such disclosure [reg.42].

New regulation 42(1)(i) extends this disclosure to fostering agencies to facilitate Fostering for Adoption.

Regulations 40–42 do not apply to section 56 information [reg.44] – see also Disclosure of Adoption Information (Post-Commencement Adoptions) Regulations 2005.

Agencies may transfer children's or adopters' records to other agencies where appropriate but must record all such transfers [reg.43(1)].

Regulation 43 provides for transfer of records to another agency.

CHILD UNDER SIX WEEKS OF AGE

Regulation 45 clarifies the application of parts of the Children Act 1989 in cases where an agency is authorised to place a child or a child under six weeks is placed for adoption.

The effect of this regulation is clarified in the statutory guidance. In summary, it removes the duty to consult parents and substitutes consultation with the adopters; it also removes the duty to promote contact and the parents' obligation to contribute to the child's maintenance [Guidance 5.11–15].

CONTACT

If an agency decides to place a child for adoption, it must consider and decide upon contact arrangements, taking into account:

- the views of the parent/guardian, and father without parental responsibility if consulted under regulation 14;
- any panel advice;
- the considerations of section 1(2) & (4) of the Act [reg.46(1)–(3)].

Agencies must notify contact arrangements to, and if proposing any change, seek and take account of the views of:

- the child (if old enough);
- if their whereabouts are known, the parent/guardian and if appropriate, a father without parental responsibility (if consulted under regulation 14);

- anyone who previously had contact under the 1989 Act; and
- any other relevant person [reg.46(4) & (6)].

Agencies must review contact arrangements after deciding to place a child in the light of the prospective adopters' views and any advice given by the panel [reg.46(5)].

Agencies must set out contact arrangements in the placement plan and keep reviewing them [reg.46(7)].

Regulation 47 provides for variation of contact under a section 26 order.

Contact may be varied by agreement with the person having contact, subject to the child's agreement (if old enough) and that of the adopters (if child placed for adoption), and after confirmation is sent to all three [reg.47(2) & (3)].

Contact may be refused under section 27(2) provided the child (if old enough), the person having contact and the adopters (if child placed) are notified immediately of the decision, date taken, reasons and duration of refusal [reg.47(1) & (3)].

Chapter 7 brings together all the Guidance in relation to contact, and highlights the possibility of unauthorised contact via social networking media [7.9].

The Adoption Support Services Regulations 2005

These regulations apply to England only and provide for local authority adoption support services.

Regulation 2 sets out definitions of terms, in particular:

- 'adoptive child' means an adopted child or where notice of intention to adopt has been given or a child who has been matched or placed for adoption;
- 'adoptive parent' means a person who has adopted, or given notice of intention to adopt, or been matched with, or had placed for adoption, a child;

Adoption Support Regulations

- 'agency adoptive child' means a child who has been adopted after an agency placement, matched or placed with adopters by an agency, or whose adoptive parent was a local authority foster carer (unless the authority opposed the adoption);
- the definition of 'related to' an adoptive child includes anyone where the relationship is judged to be beneficial to their welfare, taking account of the welfare checklist [reg.2(1)];
- financial support may continue to be paid and reviewed to adopted children who continue in full-time education after the age of 18 [reg.2(2)].

The services to be provided are:

- counselling, advice and information [s.2(6)(b) of the Act];
- financial support;
- support groups for adopters, adopted children and their birth parents/former guardians;
- assistance with contact – including mediation – between adopted children and their birth parents or relatives (includes siblings), and with others where the relationship is judged to be beneficial to the child's welfare;
- therapeutic services to adoptive children;
- services to maintain an adoption including training for adopters to meet a child's special needs and respite care (subject to the requirements on accommodating children under ss.23 or 59 Children Act 1989);
- assistance with or to prevent a disruption, including mediation and disruption meetings [reg.3(1)].

Regulation 3(3) excludes adoptions by parents, step-parents and parents' partners.

Group support, contact assistance, therapy and services to maintain adoptions may be provided by making payments [reg.3(3)].

Adoption Support Regulations

Regulation 4 sets out the entitlement of certain people to prescribed services.

The following are entitled to counselling, advice and information:

- children and their parents/guardians;
- prospective adopters;
- adoptees and their parents, birth parents/former guardians;
- adopters' children;
- those related to adoptive children (see definition under Regulation 2(2) above) including birth siblings [reg.3(2)].

Adopters of agency adoptive children are eligible for financial support [reg.3(3)].

Support groups must be provided to agency adoptive children and their adopters, birth parents/former guardians [reg.3(4)].

Contact support must be provided to agency adoptive children and their adopters, birth parents/former guardians and birth siblings [reg.3(5)].

Therapeutic services must be made available to agency adoptive children and those adopted from abroad [reg.3(6)].

Disruption support must be provided to agency adoptive children, those adopted from abroad, their adopters and any children of the adopters [reg.3(7)].

Under regulation 5, support services may be contracted out to:

- local authorities;
- adoption support agencies;
- PCTs (Health Boards);
- education authorities.

ADOPTION SUPPORT SERVICES ADVISER (ASSA)

Local authorities must appoint an 'adoption support services adviser' (ASSA) with sufficient knowledge and experience of adoption and its effect, to give advice and information about services to anyone affected by adoption [reg.6(1), (2)(a) and (3)].

The ASSA will also advise the local authority on adoption support assessments, services and plans, and liaise with other local authorities [reg.6(2)(b)].

Advice on the appointment and role of the ASSA will be found in the Guidance (9.9–16).

RESPONSIBILITY FOR SUPPORT OUTSIDE LOCAL AUTHORITY AREA

Regulation 7 makes local authorities responsible for adoption support to children they have placed outside their area, their adopters and any children of those adopters until three years after the adoption order; however, the responsibility for ongoing financial support continues as long as eligibility [reg.7(1) & (2)].

Local authorities have discretion to provide support to others outside their area as appropriate [reg.7(3)].

FINANCIAL SUPPORT

Regulation 8 provides that financial support to maintain an adoptive placement/adoption may only be paid to adopters where:

- it is necessary to ensure the child can be looked after;
- greater resources are required because of illness, disability, emotional or behavioural difficulties or the effects of abuse or neglect;
- special arrangements are necessary because of age or ethnic origin or to enable a child to be placed with a sibling or another child they have lived with;
- it is to meet regular travel costs for contact;

- as a contribution to adoption legal costs (including court fees), introductions or setting up costs, including:
  - furniture and equipment
  - adaptations to the home
  - transport
  - clothing, toys or other necessary items.

Financial support may only include a reward element:

- where the adopter was the child's foster carer; and
- the fostering allowance included a reward element [reg.9(1)].

The reward element is payable for two years from adoption (longer in exceptional circumstances at the local authority's discretion) [reg.9(2)].

Financial support is to be by way of a single payment except:

- to meet a recurring need, in which case a periodic payment (i.e. regular allowance) may be paid;
- by agreement, in instalments [reg.10].

Financial support stops when the child:

- no longer has a home with the adopter(s);
- leaves full-time education and either starts work or qualifies for income support, employment and support allowance or jobseeker's allowance (now called Universal Credit);
- reaches 18, unless continuing in full-time education, when it may continue until the end of that course [reg.11].

In order to receive periodic payments of financial support, adopters (both if a couple) must agree to:

- notify the local authority immediately (and if orally, confirm in writing in seven days) of any new address, the child's death, any changes listed in regulation 11 and any change in financial circumstances or the financial needs or resources of the child;

- supply an annual statement of financial circumstances and the financial needs and resources of the child, plus confirmation of address and that the child is still there [reg.12(1)].

Local authorities may impose conditions on payments, including how and when they are to be spent [reg.12(2)].

Payments may be suspended or stopped if any conditions are not met, and the local authority may seek repayment of part or all of the amount paid; however, in the case of failure to supply an annual statement, the authority must first send a reminder giving 28 days to comply [reg.12(3) & (4)].

A notice must be sent to the adopters (see under reg.18(3) below).

Financial support should be calculated by reference to the fostering allowance which would be payable for the particular child [Guidance 9.33].

ASSESSMENT FOR ADOPTION SUPPORT

Local authorities must assess support needs (s.4(1)(b) of the Act) at the request of:

- adopters' children;
- those related to adoptive children (see definition under reg.2(2) above) including birth siblings [reg.13(1)].

The assessment may be carried out just in relation to a particular service if the person requests it or the authority so decides [reg.13(2)].

Local authorities do not have to assess the need of people for a particular support service if they are not listed for that service in regulation 4 [reg.13(3)].

Assessments must consider any of the following which are relevant:

- the person's needs and how they might be met;
- the adoptive family's needs and how they might be met;
- child's developmental and other needs and how they might be met;

- the adopter's parenting capacity;
- family and environment;
- circumstances leading to placement for adoption;
- any previous assessments of the person's support needs [reg.14(1)].

The local authority must, if appropriate, interview the subject of any assessment, and if a child, also interview the adopter(s) [reg.14(3)].

If health or education services appear to be needed, the relevant body must be consulted as part of the assessment [reg.14(4)].

Local authorities must write a report of the assessment [reg.14(3)].

In deciding an amount of financial support, local authorities must take account of any grant, benefit, allowance or resource available to the person as an adopter [reg.15(2)].

Unless regulation 15(4) or (5) applies, local authorities must also take account of:

- the person's financial resources, including state benefits payable for the child;
- the person's reasonable outgoings and commitments (excluding the child);
- the child's financial needs and resources [reg.15(3)].

Under regulation 15(4), local authorities must disregard the means test in regulation 15(3) if paying legal costs to support an application to adopt an agency child.

Regulation 15(5) allows local authorities to disregard the regulation 15(3) means test when paying:

- setting up or special care costs for an agency child;
- ongoing travel costs for contact purposes;
- any reward element under regulation 9 (former foster carer).

Except for advice and information or one-off support, local authorities must draw up a support services plan [reg.16(2)].

If health or education services appear to be needed, the relevant body must be consulted before drawing up the plan [reg.16(3)].

Local authorities must nominate someone to monitor the plan's implementation [reg.16(4)].

People must be given the chance to make representations before a decision about support needs is made, having first been notified of the proposed decision and the time allowed for making representations [reg.17(1) & (2)].

The notice must state:

- the person's support needs;
- the basis for determining any financial support and the amount payable;
- if the local authority proposes to provide any support services, and if so which services;
- any conditions to be imposed [reg.17(3)].

If services are to be provided and a plan is required, a draft plan must accompany the notice [reg.17(4)].

No decision can be made until:

- the person has made representations or accepted the proposal and any draft plan; or
- the time limit has expired [reg.17(5)].

When the local authority has made a decision about providing support services, it must notify the person, with reasons [reg.18(1)].

If a plan is required, the notice must include the plan and the person nominated to monitor it [reg.18(2)].

For financial support, the notice must state:

- how the amount is calculated;
- the amount, frequency, period and start date of payments by instalments;
- the date of any one-off payment;
- any conditions attached, any date by which they are to be met and what happens if they are not met;
- review, variation and termination procedures;
- the local authority's and adopter's respective responsibilities with regard to payment and reviews [reg.18(3)].

REVIEWS OF ADOPTION SUPPORT

Reviews of periodic financial support are covered by regulation 20 and of other services by regulation 19.

Regulation 19(2) requires the local authority to review provision at least annually, and if the person's circumstances change, and at any other time appropriate to the plan.

Reviews must be conducted as for assessments in accordance with regulations 14 and 15 [reg.19(3)].

People must be given the chance to make representations before a decision about variation or termination of support services is made, having first been notified of the proposed decision and the time allowed for making representations. The notice must contain the information listed in regulation 17(3) and any revised draft plan [reg.19(4) & (5)].

Local authorities must make a decision about variation or termination based on the review and any representations, and if necessary revise the plan; they must then notify the person, with reasons and details of any revised plan [reg.19(6) & (7)].

Regulation 20(2) requires local authorities to review financial support on receipt of the annual statement, and if the person's circumstances change or any condition is breached, and at any other time appropriate to the plan.

Reviews must be conducted as for assessments in accordance with regulations 14 and 15 [reg.20(4)].

People must be given the chance to make representations before a decision to reduce or stop payments or revise the plan, having first been notified of the proposed decision and the time allowed for making representations. The notice must contain the information listed in regulation 17(3) and any revised draft plan [reg.20(5) & (7)].

Payments may be suspended pending a decision [reg.20(6)].

Local authorities must make a decision about variation, termination or recovery of any payments made, based on the review and any representations, and if necessary revise the plan; they must then notify the person, with reasons and details of any revised plan [reg.20(8) & (9)].

In urgent cases, the local authority may disregard any requirement to assess, plan or notify which would delay service provision [reg.21].

Regulation 22 requires notices to be in writing, and in the case of a child who is not of sufficient age or understanding or where the local authority deems it inappropriate, to be given to the adopter or other appropriate adult.

Regulation 23 enables area local authorities providing support services (except advice and information) to recover their costs from placing local authorities unless that authority is required to provide services under regulation 7.

Assessments, plans, reviews and support services under the 2003 Regulations on 30.12.05 are treated as effective under these Regulations.

There is detailed Guidance in Chapter 9 on all aspects of adoption support provision, including useful clarification on division of responsibility between local authorities.

Independent Review Regulations

The Independent Review of Determinations (Adoption & Fostering) Regulations 2009

These regulations apply to England only and in relation to adoption implement section 12 of the Act. They cover two types of adoption agency decisions:

- not to approve a prospective adopter under the Adoption Agencies Regulations 2005 (a 'suitability determination');
- not to disclose information in accordance with the Disclosure of Adoption Information (Post-commencement adoptions) Regulations 2005 (a 'disclosure determination') [reg.1–3].

Guidance on the independent review mechanism is found in Chapter 1, paragraphs 64–81 of the Adoption Guidance.

Regulation 5 provides for the setting up of panels to review applications received by the Secretary of State. Membership of the panel is drawn from a central list maintained by the Secretary of State to include:

- social workers (with three years post-qualifying child care experience, including direct adoption experience);
- social workers (with three years post-qualifying child care experience, including direct fostering experience);
- registered medical practitioners; and
- others, including where practicable people with personal experience of adoption and those who have been local authority foster carers within the last two years.

The Secretary of State appoints a suitably experienced Chair, and for a suitability case, one of the members as vice-chair [reg.9].

The following are prohibited from being on the panel:

- any member of the panel which made the decision being reviewed;
- elected members of or those employed for the purposes of adoption, child protection or child placement by a local authority which made the qualifying determination;

Independent Review Regulations

- employees or trustees of a voluntary agency which made the qualifying determination;
- foster carers approved by the agency;
- adopters of a child placed by the agency unless more than a year after the adoption order;
- anyone adopted or fostered through the agency;
- anyone with personal or professional knowledge of the applicant [reg.10].

Regulation 10(2)(a) defines 'employed' as paid or voluntary and direct or as a contractor.

Regulation 11 provides for panels reviewing a suitability case in adoption.

The panel must take account of all information provided, may request other information or assistance from the agency and may take legal advice [reg.11(5)].

The panel must review the decision and make a recommendation to the agency. The recommendation can be that:

- the applicant is suitable to adopt a child (if the prospective adopter's report complied with regulation 30, Adoption Agencies Regulations);
- the agency should prepare a report which complies with regulation 30, Adoption Agencies Regulations;
- the applicant is not suitable to adopt a child [reg.11(2)–(4)].

Regulation 12 provides for panels reviewing a disclosure case.

The panel must review the decision and recommend whether or not the agency should proceed with its original decision [reg.12(2)].

The panel must take account of all information provided, may request other information or assistance from the agency and may take legal advice [reg.12(3)].

Regulation 13 provides for panels reviewing fostering determinations.

Panel members may be paid reasonable fees [reg.14].

The quorum for a suitability panel meeting is five, including the Chair or vice-chair and a social worker with the relevant experience in adoption or fostering [reg.15(2)].

For a disclosure panel, the quorum is three including at least two social workers with the prescribed experience in adoption [reg.15(1)].

Records are to be kept securely for 12 months and must include the reasons for the recommendation and whether it was a unanimous or majority recommendation [reg.16].

An application for a panel review must be in writing and state the grounds for applying [reg.17].

The application will be acknowledged and a copy sent to the agency. A panel will be set up and the applicant and agency will be notified of the arrangements. Applicants have until three weeks before the meeting to provide further written details and may also address the panel [reg.18].

The agency must provide any information or assistance requested by the panel if reasonably practicable [reg.19].

The panel's recommendation may be a majority decision [reg.20(1)].

The panel record must give reasons for the recommendation, state whether it is unanimous or by a majority, be signed and dated by the Chair and be sent to the applicant and the agency without delay [reg.20(2) & (3)].

The panel may order the agency to pay reasonable costs [reg.21].

The Adoptions with a Foreign Element Regulations 2005

These regulations make provision relating to adoptions with a foreign element under the Adoption (Intercountry Aspects) Act 1999 and the 2002 Act. They supplement and should be read in conjunction with the Adoption Agencies Regulations 2005.

The Guidance on intercountry adoption is being revised. In the meantime, further information on adoptions with a foreign element, including flowcharts showing the procedure to be followed in, and tables setting out the immigration requirements for different types of adoption, is to be found in Annex C of the 2005 Adoption Guidance which remains in force.

BRINGING A CHILD TO THE UK

Regulation 3 requires anyone who intends to bring a child to the UK for adoption (or adopted overseas in the last 12 months) to apply in writing for assessment by an adoption agency and to supply any information required for the assessment.

Before bringing a child into the UK, a prospective adopter must have received a notice from the Secretary of State that a certificate has been issued to the overseas authority confirming:

- their approval and eligibility to adopt;
- that a child if adopted and granted entry clearance will have permanent right of residence in the UK [reg.4(2)(a)].

The prospective adopter(s) must visit a child in the country of origin before bringing them to the UK [reg.4(2)(c)] and afterwards:

- confirm the visit and intention to proceed, in writing, to the agency;
- provide any additional reports or information;
- notify the agency of the expected date when the child will be brought to the UK [reg.4(2)(d)].

Before visiting the child overseas, a prospective adopter must:

- provide the adoption agency with any reports and information received about the child;
- discuss with the agency the proposed match [reg.4(2)(b)].

Regulation 4(3) requires the adopter(s) to accompany the child to the UK unless the agency and the overseas authority agree only one of a couple needs to do so.

Foreign Element Regulations

Unless the child is adopted or to be adopted in an overseas adoption, the prospective adopter must notify their local authority within 14 days of:

- the child's arrival in the UK; and
- the prospective adopter's intention to apply to adopt (or not to keep the child) [reg.4(4)].

If the prospective adopter subsequently moves to a new area, they must notify the new local authority within 14 days [reg.4(5)].

Once notified, the local authority must:

- set up a file containing information from the overseas authority, adoption agency, prospective adopter, entry clearance officer and Secretary of State/Welsh Parliament [reg.5(1)(a)];
- notify the prospective adopter's GP and PCT/Local Health Board and send any health information to the GP [reg.5(1)(b) & (c)];
- notify the education authority if the child is of school age, and send any educational information, including the likelihood of an assessment of special educational needs [reg.5(1)(d)];
- visit the child and the prospective adopter within one week; then at least weekly until the first review; and at its discretion thereafter until the child moves or is adopted; and in each visit advise on adoption support services as necessary [reg.5(1)(e) & (h)(iii)];
- review the case within four weeks of the notice, three months after the first review if necessary and at six-monthly intervals thereafter until the child moves or is adopted [reg.5(1)(f)];
- advise on the child's needs, welfare and development [reg.5(1)(h)(i)].

Reviews must consider the child's needs, welfare and development and any changes required, adoption support and if reassessment is needed, and the need for further reviews [reg.5(1)(g)].

Written reports of all visits and reviews must be placed on the child's file [reg.5(1)(h)(ii)].

Files must comply with Part 7 of the Adoption Agencies Regulations or the Welsh equivalent [reg.5(2)].

The local authority must review the case if no application is made within two years, and consider:

- the child's needs, welfare and development and any necessary changes;
- the exercise of parental responsibility;
- entry terms and immigration status;
- adoption support and if a reassessment is needed;
- with other agencies, health and education [reg.5(3) & (4)].

If notified that a prospective adopter will move or has moved to another local authority area, a local authority must notify the new authority within 14 days and send full details, including the date of the original notice of intention to adopt [reg.5(5)].

Regulations 6–9 clarify the application of Chapter 3 of the 2002 Act to intercountry adoption cases in relation to removal [reg.6]; change of name and removal from the UK [reg.7]; return of the child [reg.8]; and period of time the child must live with the adopter(s), which is:

- six months if requirements have been met; or
- 12 months if not [reg.9].

Regulation 10 sets out the conditions to be met in cases where a parental responsibility order is sought to enable a child to be taken abroad for adoption (s.84 of the Act).

Regulation 11 extends certain provisions of the Act relating to adoption orders to section 84 orders.

HAGUE CONVENTION ADOPTIONS – BRITISH APPLICANTS

Regulations 12–34 inclusive apply to Hague Convention adoptions of children from overseas by British applicants.

Prospective adopters must:

- be 21 or over;
- have lived in the UK for a year;
- apply in writing to an agency for an assessment;
- give any information required for the assessment [reg.13].

Unless satisfied that another agency has done so, agencies must counsel applicants in accordance with regulation 24 Adoption Agencies Regulations and also give them verbal and written information about adopting from their chosen country [reg.14].

The requirements of regulations 21–30F Adoption Agencies Regulations apply in relation to checks, preparation, assessment, approval and recordkeeping. The prospective adopter's report must cover:

- proposed state of origin;
- eligibility to adopt from that country;
- information required for that country; and
- suitability to adopt from that country [reg.15].

The agency must make a decision in accordance with regulation 30B Adoption Agencies Regulations [reg.16].

Approval must be reviewed annually until a child is matched under regulation 30D Adoption Agencies Regulations [reg.17].

In Hague Convention cases, all documentation must be sent by the agency to the UK Central Authority, which will pass it on to the Central Authority in the State of Origin, and write to the agency and the adopter confirming this has been done [reg.18].

The overseas Central Authority will send information about a matched child to the UK Central Authority, which must pass it on to the agency [reg.19(1)].

The agency must consider the proposed match, send the information to the adopter(s) and meet them to discuss it and appropriate support, and if necessary counsel them [reg.19(2)].

The adopter(s) must write to confirm an intention to proceed with adoption; the agency must notify the UK Central Authority in writing that this has been done and that it is in agreement [reg.19(3)].

The UK Central Authority then notifies the overseas Central Authority of the adopter's wish to proceed and its agreement, and confirms authority for the child to enter and live in the UK [reg.19(4)].

The adopter(s) and the agency must be informed when the two Central Authorities have reached agreement [reg.19(5)].

If the overseas Central Authority decides not to proceed with the match, the UK Central Authority informs the agency which informs the adopter(s); if the agency reviews the adopter(s) and decides they are no longer suitable, or if the adopter(s) withdraw, the agency informs the UK Central Authority which informs the overseas Central Authority; in all cases the information on the child must be returned to the overseas Central Authority [reg.20].

The adopter(s) must notify the agency when they propose to bring the child to the UK, confirm when the child is placed and accompany the child to the UK (both adopters unless the agency and the overseas Central Authority agree only one of a couple needs to do so) [reg.21].

Before the child enters the UK, the agency must notify the prospective adopter's GP and PCT/Local Health Board and send any health information to the GP, notify the local authority (if not the agency), and notify the education authority if the child is of school age, and send any educational information, including the likelihood of an assessment of special educational needs [reg.22].

If a child is brought to the UK in a Hague Convention case without first being adopted abroad, the prospective adopter must notify their local authority within 14 days of the child's arrival in the UK, and the prospective adopter's intention to apply to adopt (or not to keep the child), and if the prospective adopter moves, must also notify the new local authority within 14 days of moving [reg.24].

A local authority notified under regulation 24 must comply with the requirements of regulation 5 as for non-Convention cases [reg.25].

If the adopter notifies a local authority that they do not wish to proceed with the adoption, the child must be returned within seven days and the local authority must notify the UK Central Authority [reg.26].

If a local authority decides the placement is not in the child's best interests, it must notify the adopter(s) and the UK Central Authority; the adopter(s) must return the child within seven days, subject to any order of a court where an adoption application is pending [reg.27].

Regulation 28 requires local authorities to arrange new adoptive placements for children who are returned or removed, or where a Convention adoption order is refused or annulled (provided the local authority is satisfied it is in the child's best interests). If the local authority is not satisfied that another UK placement is in the child's best interests, it must liaise with the UK Central Authority to arrange their return overseas. In either case, the local authority must consider the child's wishes and feelings (subject to age and understanding) and obtain their consent if appropriate.

Local authorities must comply with any request for a report in cases where a child is brought to the UK under a Convention adoption order which is subject to a probationary period, and the report must contain the requested information and be submitted on time [reg.29].

Regulation 30 specifies additional information for Hague Convention cases to be included in a court report under section 44(5) of the Act.

Regulation 31 sets out the requirements for the making of a Convention adoption order:

- the applicant, or both applicants if a couple, must have been habitually resident in the UK for at least a year;
- the child was previously resident in a Convention country overseas; and
- if neither of the applicants is a British citizen, the child has been authorised to enter and live in the UK.

The UK Central Authority must issue a Schedule 2 certificate when a Convention adoption order is made in England or Wales and send it to the overseas Central Authority, the adopter(s), the agency and (if different) the local authority [reg.32(1)].

When a Convention adoption order is made overseas, the UK Central Authority will receive a certificate and must send a copy to the adopter(s), the agency and (if different) the local authority [reg.32(2)].

If a Convention adoption application is withdrawn or refused, the adopter must return the child to the local authority when directed by the Court [reg.33].

An order annulling a Convention adoption will be sent to the UK Central Authority which must send a copy to the overseas Central Authority [reg.34].

HAGUE CONVENTION ADOPTIONS – OVERSEAS APPLICANTS

Regulations 35–51 inclusive apply to Hague Convention adoptions of British children by overseas adopters.

Unless satisfied that another agency has done so, an agency must in Convention cases comply with the requirements of regulations 13 (counselling and information for the child) and 14 (counselling and information for the parents) Adoption Agencies Regulations, including additional information about Convention adoption [regs.36 & 37].

The child's permanence report (reg.17, Adoption Agencies Regulations) must include assessment of whether a child could be adopted in the UK and if adoption overseas is in their best interests. The report must be sent to the panel together with any reports received from overseas and the agency's comments on them, and the panel must consider these [regs.38 & 39].

Agencies which make a decision to place a child for a Convention adoption must send full details to the UK Central Authority (which will keep a list) and to notify the Central Authority if the child is placed in the UK or the best interests decision is changed [regs.40 & 41].

UK Central Authorities will match children on the list with prospective adopters in overseas Convention countries who meet the requirements (unless the adopter has been identified for a named child) and notify the referring local authority [reg.42].

The agency and panel must consider whether the proposed placement should proceed, and the panel must consider any reports and information sent [regs.43 & 44].

The requirements of reg.33(3) Adoption Agencies Regulations to notify the adopters and the child's parents of its decision do not apply, but the agency must notify the UK Central Authority as soon as possible, and if not agreeing to the placement, return all documents to the UK Central Authority for return to the overseas Central Authority [reg.45].

If agreeing to the placement, the agency must prepare a report covering the information required by Schedule 1 Adoption Agencies Regulations (in effect, a child's permanence report) and send it, together with details of any court orders and confirmation of parental consent, to the UK Central Authority to be passed to the overseas Central Authority [reg.46].

The UK Central Authority can agree to the proposed placement provided that:

- the adopters have agreed to proceed, have visited the child and have agreed to travel with the child;
- adopters in Convention cases have been advised to apply for a parental responsibility order (s.84(1) of the Act);
- the child will have the right of entry and residence in the receiving state [reg.47(1)–(2) & (4)].

Agencies may not place the child until advised by the UK Central Authority that agreement has been reached [reg.47(3)].

CONDITIONS FOR A PARENTAL RESPONSIBILITY ORDER UNDER S.84

The relevant overseas bodies must prepare a report on the adopters, confirm their eligibility, counsel them and confirm the child's eligibility to enter and live in the receiving state.

The UK agency must prepare a report on the child; comply with the Adoption Agencies Regulations and these Regulations; supply the court with the child's permanence report, the panel's recommendations and the adoption placement report; include in its court report (ss.43(a), 44(5) of the Act) details of any visits and reviews, and in a Convention case, copies of the required Convention reports and agreement.

The adopters have agreed in writing to travel with the child (unless agreed that only one of a couple need do so) [regs.48 & 49].

CONVENTION ADOPTION ORDERS

Convention adoption orders can only be made if:

- the adopters (both if a couple) have lived in the receiving state for a year;
- the child was resident in the UK when the agreement was made;
- the child's right to enter and remain in the receiving state has been confirmed [reg.50].

When a UK Central Authority receives a Convention adoption order, it must issue a Schedule 2 Certificate and send it to the overseas Central Authority and the local authority, and if it receives a certificate issued by another UK Central Authority it must send that to the local authority [reg.51].

Regulation 52 provides that the Act (as modified in the succeeding regulations) applies to Convention adoptions unless clearly contradictory.

Regulations 53–58 make minor modifications to certain sections of the Act for the purpose of Convention adoptions.

Regulation 59 makes it an offence to fail to notify the local authority under regulation 24 or comply with a requirement to return a child under regulations 26, 27 or 33.

The Adopted Children and Adoption Contact Registers Regulations 2005

These regulations govern the operation of the Adopted Children Register and the Adoption Contact Register.

Details of agency duties to those seeking intermediary services or access to information is found in Guidance Chapter 12.

Regulation 2 prescribes the form for entries in the Adopted Children Register as set out in Schedule 1 (England) and Schedule 2 (Wales).

Under regulation 3, foreign adoptions are registrable if the adopter (or both adopters if a couple) is habitually resident in England or Wales.

Regulation 4 provides that an application to register a child adopted under a registrable foreign adoption may be made by:

- the adopter (or one of them);
- anyone with parental responsibility;
- the adopted person if over 18.

An application must be in writing and accompanied by prescribed documents and other information [reg.5(1) & (2)].

Applicants must arrange for documents which are not in English or Welsh to be translated into English [reg.5(4)].

Regulation 6 prescribes the information to be held in Part 1 of the Register (and Schedule 3 the form):

- adoptee's name, address and date of birth;

The Registers Regulations

- relatives (named if known) that the person does or does not wish to have contact with.

Regulation 7 prescribes the information to be held in Part 2 of the Register (and Schedule 4 the form):

- the relative's name, address and date of birth;
- the name of the adoptee they wish to have contact with; or
- their wish not to have contact with a named adoptee.

Regulation 8 requires the Registrar General to give an adoptee named in Part 1 of the Register the name and contact address for any relative named in Part 2 of the Register who wishes to have contact.

Regulation 9 lays down fees of £15 for Part 1 of the Register (adoptees) and £30 for Part 2 (relatives).

Regulation 10 specifies that applicants for certified copies of entries in the Adopted Children Register relating to adopted children (i.e. under 18), must supply the:

- adopted child's full name and date of birth;
- adopter's/adopters' full name/s.

An appropriate adoption agency (defined in s.65(1) of the Act) must apply in writing for information from the Register enabling an adoptee to obtain a copy of their birth certificate [reg.11].

Regulation 12 applies to pre-commencement adoptions and requires written applications for information necessary to enable adoptees over 18 to obtain a copy of their birth certificate.

Regulation 13 requires written applications for such information by adoptees under 18 who intend to marry or form a civil partnership.

Regulation 14 revokes previous regulations, except the Forms of Adoption Entry Regulations 1975 for pre-commencement adoptions, and the Registration of Foreign Adoption Regulations 2003 for certain intercountry adoptions.

The Adoption Information Regulations

The Adoption Information and Intermediary Services (Pre-Commencement Adoptions) Regulations 2005

These regulations apply in England only and deal with assisting people adopted before 30.12.05 ('pre-commencement') to obtain information about their adoption and to facilitate contact with their birth relatives and to facilitate contact between birth relatives and people with a prescribed relationship with the adopted person.

Note that the Regulations were amended by the Adoption Information and Intermediary Services (Pre-Commencement Adoptions) (Amendment) Regulations 2014, but that the Regulations have not, at the time of writing, been updated on the legislation.gov.uk website.

The Adoption Agencies Regulations 1983 continue to apply in relation to retention of case records for pre-commencement adoptions.

Disclosure of information about adoptions on or after 30.12.05 is dealt with by the Disclosure of Adoption Information (Post-Commencement Adoptions) Regulations 2005.

Guidance on adoption records and the application of the Data Protection Act is given in Chapters 6 (before adoption) and 11 (after adoption) of the Statutory Guidance on Adoption 2013.

Reference should be made to Chapter 10 of the Guidance and the Practice Guidance Adoption: Access to Information and Intermediary Services.

INTERMEDIARY SERVICES AND INTERMEDIARY AGENCIES

In these Regulations, 'adopted person' refers only to an adult adopted before 30 December 2005 [reg 2].

Intermediary services are defined by regulation 4 as:

- assisting adopted people over 18 who were adopted pre-commencement to obtain information about their adoption;
- facilitating contact with their relatives; and
- facilitating contact between persons with a prescribed relationship to an adopted person and relatives of the adopted person.

Adoption agencies which placed a person for adoption or hold their adoption information, and local authorities to which notice of a non-agency adoption was given are referred to as 'the appropriate adoption agency' and are not deemed to be providing intermediary services if they only provide information on the adoption to that person [reg.4(2)].

Adoption agencies and registered adoption support agencies providing intermediary services are 'intermediary agencies' for the purpose of the regulations [reg.4(3)].

Regulation 3 stipulates that only adoption agencies and registered adoption support agencies may provide intermediary services and must do so in accordance with these regulations [reg.3(1) & (2)].

Intermediary services are classed as an adoption support service [reg.3(3)].

Intermediary agencies may accept applications to assist people adopted before 30.12.05 and their relatives to make contact, provided that both the applicant and the person with whom they seek contact are over 18 [reg.5(3)]. If the agency learns at any time that the subject of the application is under 18, it must not proceed further [reg.6(4)].

An intermediary agency must not proceed with an application:

- from a birth relative if a veto applies;
- from a person with a prescribed relationship if a veto applies, unless that person is a spouse/civil partner, child, grandchild or great grandchild of the adopted person who is only seeking family medical history;
- from a person with a prescribed relationship if the adopted person does not consent, unless the intermediary service has taken all reasonable steps to locate the adopted person but has been unable to do so [reg.5A].

Intermediary agencies are not required to proceed with applications if it would not be appropriate, having regard to:

The Adoption Information Regulations

- the welfare of the applicant, the subject [reg.6(2)(a)(i) & (ii)] and anyone who may be identified or affected (in particular anyone aged under 18 [reg.6(2)(a)(iii) & (3)]);
- the views of the adoption agency [reg.6(2)(b)];
- information obtained from the Adoption Contact Register [reg.6(2)(c)];
- all the circumstances of the case [reg.6(2)].

CONSENT

Agencies are required to obtain the subject's consent before disclosing identifying information [reg.7(1)]. Identifying information is defined as that which on its own or with other known information enables the subject to be identified or traced [reg.7(4)].

The agency must take all reasonable steps to obtain informed consent [reg.7(3)].

If the subject is dead or incapable of giving informed consent, the agency may disclose identifying information if appropriate [reg.7(2) and 6(2)].

VETO ON CONTACT

Regulation 8 enables an adoptee to write to register a veto with the appropriate agency preventing contact from intermediary agencies, or contact except in specified circumstances [reg.8(1)].

A veto registered by an adopted person will apply to an application where the subject of the application is a person with a prescribed relationship to the adopted person. Any veto made before the extension of the provisions to persons with a prescribed relationship is deemed to apply to any application made.

The agency must record the veto on the adoptee's file and inform any intermediary agency which makes contact [reg.8(2)].

Intermediary agencies must not proceed with an application if aware of a veto, except in the specified circumstances [reg.8(3)].

If the subject has not consented or a veto applies, non-identifying information may still be disclosed if the agency considers it appropriate [reg.9].

COUNSELLING

Intermediary agencies must provide written information about counselling, including providers and costs, to applicants and to subjects considering whether or not to consent, and must arrange it if requested [reg.10(1), (2) & (3)].

Regulation 10(4) defines agencies which may provide counselling.

Intermediary agencies must confirm the applicant's identity and age, that anyone acting for the applicant is authorised, and that any relative applying is related to the subject [reg.11].

Intermediary agencies (unless the appropriate adoption agency) must take steps to identify any adoption agency which was involved in the adoption, including:

- writing to the Registrar General;
- writing to the court which made the order;
- approaching the local authority where the adoption took place [reg.12(1) & (2)].

The intermediary agency must then contact the identified adoption agency to find out if the subject has registered a veto or expressed any view about contact; seek the agency's views on the application; and ask for the information necessary to trace the subject, enable them to make an informed decision about consent, and provide counselling to the subject and the applicant [reg.12(3)].

The appropriate adoption agency must provide the information requested unless a veto applies [reg.12(4)].

Disclosure Regulations

The intermediary agency may make a request to the Registrar General for information about:

- the identity of the appropriate adoption agency;
- details of the court that made the adoption order;
- information that would enable an application for a copy of the adopted person's adoption certificate or birth certificate;
- information from the Adoption Contact Register [reg.13].

The Registrar General must take reasonable steps to comply with the request [reg.14].

The court must comply with any ensuing request or if it does not have the information, supply details of any other court that may hold the information [reg.15].

Regulation 16 requires information obtained or held under these regulations to be treated as confidential, and only disclosed in prescribed circumstances.

Regulation 17 makes it an offence for an intermediary agency to disclose information without the subject's consent.

Regulation 18 permits intermediary agencies and adoption agencies to charge reasonable fees.

The Registrar General may charge £36 for processing an initial request for information and £14 for providing information in response to any subsequent request under regulation 13 [reg.18(3)].

Courts may charge intermediary agencies up to £20 for providing information under regulation 15 [reg.18(4)].

The Disclosure of Adoption Information (Post-Commencement Adoptions) Regulations 2005

These regulations apply in England only and cover information to be kept by agencies and applications for disclosure of information relating to adoptions on or after 30.12.05 ('post-commencement').

Assistance with obtaining information about adoptions before 30.12.05 is dealt with by the Adoption Information and Intermediary Services (Pre-Commencement Adoptions) Regulations 2005.

Guidance on adoption records and the application of the Data Protection Act is given in Chapters 6 (before adoption) and 11 (after adoption) of the Statutory Guidance.

Reference should be made to Chapter 11 of the Guidance and the Practice Guidance Adoption: Access to Information and Intermediary Services.

The adoption agency which placed the child or holds the records of the adoption [reg.3] must keep prescribed records, known as 's.56 information', including the file set up in accordance with the Adoption Agencies Regulations 1983 or 2005 [reg.4(1) & (2)].

Unless prejudicial to the adopted person's welfare or not reasonably practicable [reg.4(4)], the agency must keep:

- anything supplied by a birth parent, relative or other significant person and intended to be given to the adopted person on request;
- anything the adopted person has asked to be kept;
- information from the Registrar General;
- information from the Adoption Contact Register;
- records made in compliance with regulations 10, 11, 14 & 18 (see below) [reg.4(3)].

Section 56 information must be kept securely for at least 100 years after the adoption order, and be protected from theft, unauthorised disclosure, damage, loss and destruction [regs.5 & 6].

Regulation 7 provides for transfer of section 56 records on cessation of an agency's activity to another agency (with approval of the registration authority), to the local authority where the agency (or its head office) is based, or to the resulting new agency if amalgamating. A voluntary agency must notify the local authority where most activity took place of the transfer. The receiving agency must notify the registration authority.

Regulation 8 permits agencies to disclose section 56 information except 'protected information' (s.57(3) 2002 Act) for the purposes of carrying out its duties, and including protected information to another agency or support agency carrying out disclosure work, or to a researcher authorised by the Secretary of State.

Regulation 9 requires agencies to disclose section 56 information (including protected information) in various prescribed circumstances.

Agencies must record any information disclosed under regulations 8 or 9, including what was disclosed, when, to whom and why [reg.10].

Regulation 11 provides for agreements as to the disclosure of protected information between an agency and:

- anyone 18 or over in relation to information about them [reg.11(1)(a)].
- adopters or parents who had parental responsibility before the adoption in relation to information about them or about the adopted person [reg.11(1)(b)].

Agreements must be in writing and include the names and signatures of the parties, the date, the reason for the agreement, and the information to be disclosed or any restrictions on the circumstances in which it may be disclosed [reg.11(2)].

An agency receiving an application for disclosure of protected information – which must be in writing and give reasons [reg.12] – must try to confirm the applicant's identity and that anyone acting on their behalf is authorised [reg.13].

Any views on disclosure obtained by the agency must be recorded [reg.14].

The following agency decisions are 'qualifying determinations' for the purposes of the Independent Review Mechanism (s.12 2002 Act):

- not to proceed with a disclosure application;
- to disclose information against the subject's wishes;

- not to disclose to the applicant information a person wishes to be disclosed [reg.15(1)].

The agency must advise the person in writing of the decision, the reasons for it, and the procedure for seeking an independent review [reg.15(2)].

On being notified of an application to the IRM, the agency must send to the Secretary of State within 10 working days:

- a copy of the disclosure application;
- a copy of the notice of its determination;
- a record of any views obtained by the agency;
- any other information the panel requests [reg.15(3)].

The agency must not act on its decision until the IRM panel has made a recommendation (and must take account of that recommendation before proceeding [reg.15(5)]) or for 40 days if no IRM application is made [reg.15(4)].

Regulations 15(6) and 15(7) clarify the definition of various terms.

Agencies must provide written information about available counselling and any fees charged to applicants for disclosure of information; anyone whose views about disclosure have been sought; and anyone making or considering an agreement under regulation 11, and arrange it on request [regs.16 & 17(1)].

Counselling may be provided by:

- the agency itself;
- an adoption agency or adoption support agency if the person is in England and Wales; a Scottish adoption agency if in Scotland; a registered adoption society or Board (defined by reg.17(3)) if in Northern Ireland; or an equivalent person or body if outside the UK [reg.17(2)].

Agencies may disclose information (including protected information) to a counsellor it has arranged under regulation 17, but must record any such disclosure in writing [reg.18].

If an agency does not hold information sought by an applicant over 18 who wishes to obtain a copy of their birth certificate, the agency must apply (paying any fee [reg.20(2)]) to the Registrar General for it, by supplying:

- the adoptee's name, date and country of birth;
- the adopters' names;
- the date of the adoption order [reg.19].

Regulation 20 requires the Registrar General to disclose information required for a person to contact an adoption agency that holds their adoption records, and to disclose information from the Adoption Contact Register if asked by an agency dealing with a disclosure application.

Regulation 21 creates an offence by a voluntary agency of disclosing information in contravention of section 57 of the 2002 Act.

Regulation 22 permits agencies to charge reasonable fees for disclosing information; for providing counselling about disclosure; or for arranging such counselling outside the UK provided it has first given information about fees [reg.21(1) & (3)]; however, no fee may be charged to an adoptee for disclosure of information about their relatives and counselling connected with such disclosure [reg.21(2)].

The Restriction on the Preparation of Adoption Reports Regulations 2005

These regulations impose restrictions on the preparation of adoption reports under section 94(1) of the 2002 Act.

Under regulation 3, those permitted to prepare adoption reports for the purposes of section 94(1) are:

- social workers employed by an adoption agency who have at least three years' post-qualification child care experience including adoption, or supervised by an employee who meets this requirement; or
- student social workers employed by or placed with an adoption agency and supervised by an employee who meets the experience requirement; or
- social workers acting on the agency's behalf with the prescribed experience and supervised by an employee who meets the experience requirement.

The interpretation of 'direct experience of adoption' is set out in the Guidance 1.13.

The reports covered by the restrictions are:

- a child's permanence report;
- a prospective adopter's report;
- an adoption placement report;
- a report of an adoption placement visit (domestic adoptions);
- a report of a visit or review (intercountry adoptions);
- pre- and post-adoption reports;
- court reports on agency and non-agency cases, and on applications for parental responsibility prior to adoption abroad [reg.4].

The Suitability of Adopters Regulations 2005

These regulations apply in England only and prescribe the matters an agency must take into account in determining the suitability of a prospective adopter.

Except where regulation 5 applies (see below), regulation 3 requires agencies to take account of the following in preparing prospective adopter's reports and review reports:

Suitability of Adopters Regulations

- pre-assessment counselling;
- preparation;
- enhanced CRB check (now called DBS check);
- information required by Schedule 4 Part 1 Adoption Agencies Regulations 2005;
- if applicable, any additional information about adopting from abroad (reg.15(4) Adoptions with a Foreign Element Regulations 2005);
- medical report;
- referee interview reports;
- report from the adopter's local authority.

Except where regulation 5 applies (see below), agencies are required to take account of the following in reaching a decision as to a prospective adopter's suitability:

- prospective adopter's report;
- medical report;
- referee interview reports;
- panel recommendation;
- any additional information requested by the panel;
- if applicable, information about adopting from abroad (Part 3 Chapter 1 Adoptions with a Foreign Element Regulations 2005) [reg.4(1)].

In deciding on a couple's suitability, agencies must have proper regard to the stability and permanence of their relationship [reg.4(2)].

Regulation 5 applies where an agency receives information suggesting a prospective adopter may be unsuitable; in this case the agency may make a brief report and decision based only on the information collected up to that point (reg.30(4) Adoption Agencies Regulations 2005).

Adoption Support Agencies (England) and Adoption Agencies (Miscellaneous Amendments) Regulations 2005

These regulations apply in England only and cover the provision of adoption support services by adoption support agencies under the Act, and for their regulation under the Care Standards Act 2000. Minor amendments to the Adoption Agencies Regulations 1983 (applicable only before 30.12.05) and the Adoption Information and Intermediary Services (Pre-commencement Adoptions) Regulations 2005 were included. The Regulations have been amended twice, in 2010 and in 2023.

Regulation 2(2) clarifies that the term 'employee' covers volunteers and unpaid as well as paid workers.

Regulation 3 defines adoption support services as:

- counselling, advice and information;
- services for adoptions by parents and their partners including support groups, help with contact, therapy, training and respite (if including accommodation, subject to sections 23 or 59 Children Act 1989 [reg.3(2)]) and other services which maintain the adoption, and help with or to prevent disruption;
- helping agencies prepare and train adopters;
- help with contact for adopted adults and their relatives and former relatives.

Regulation 4 excludes from being considered adoption support agencies:

- lawyers providing a service as part of their practice;
- anyone just running adoption groups;
- registered homes or agencies providing respite or day care including as adoption support;

- a person providing adoption support services only under contract from an adoption agency or adoption support agency.

The Adoption Support Agencies (England) (Amendment) Regulations 2023 came into force on 18 December 2023 and provides a further exception for the provision of counselling in relation to adoption to an adult [reg 4(4)].

Adoption support agencies are required to produce and review a Statement of Purpose and (if services are provided to children) a Children's Guide and provide copies for the registration authority, staff and service users. The Children's Guide must be in a form suitable for the comprehension and ages of children served by the agency. The agency must act in accordance with its Statement of Purpose [regs.5 & 6].

A person running an agency must:

- be of good character, physically and mentally fit;
- not be bankrupt;
- supply the checks, references and information listed in Schedule 2 [reg.7].

Organisations or partnerships, or anyone unfit or not wishing to run the agency, must appoint a suitably qualified and experienced manager who meets the requirements, and advise the registration authority [regs.8 & 9].

The person running the agency must do so with care, competence and skill, and must undertake regular training [reg.10].

Regulation 11 requires the manager or person running the agency to supply written details of any criminal conviction immediately to the registration authority.

Agencies providing services to children must have a child protection policy and procedure which includes:

- what to do about allegations of abuse or neglect;

- liaison and co-operation with local authorities;
- how to contact relevant local authorities and the registration authority about any concern [reg.12].

Regulation 13 requires services to be appropriate to the person's assessed needs.

Regulation 14 stipulates the information to be held in records and allows the agency discretion as to how long to maintain them.

Adoption support agencies holding records of pre-commencement adoptions (before 30.12.05) have the same obligations as adoption agencies in relation to storage, retention, transfer and disclosure of information from those records [reg.15].

Agencies must have a complaints procedure for service users (including people refused a service) and must supply a copy to staff, and on request to service users and anyone acting on a child's behalf [reg.16].

Complaints must be fully investigated, within 28 days where practicable, and the complainant advised of the outcome and any resulting action [reg.17(1) & (2)].

Records of the complaint, investigation, outcome and action taken must be kept for three years [reg.17(3)].

Agencies must enable children to complain, and ensure there are no reprisals for making a complaint [reg.17(4)].

Agencies must supply the registration authority on request a summary of the previous year's complaints and action taken [reg.17(5)].

Agencies must have enough suitably qualified and experienced staff for their statement of purpose and to meet the needs of services users [reg.18].

Staff must:

- be of good character, physically and mentally fit; have the necessary qualifications, skills and experience; supply the checks, references and information listed in Schedule 2 [reg.19];

- be appointed subject to a probationary period; given a job description; receive training, supervision and appraisal; be enabled to gain appropriate further qualifications [reg.20].

Agencies must have a disciplinary procedure, which includes suspension of staff to safeguard service users, and makes it a disciplinary matter not to report actual or suspected abuse of a child [reg.21].

Agencies must keep staff records covering the information specified in Schedule 3 for a period of at least 15 years from date of last entry [reg.22].

Premises must be suitable to the agency's statement of purpose and must provide secure storage for records; records stored off the premises must also be kept securely [reg.23].

Regulation 24 requires the agency to notify the bodies set out in Schedule 4 of the death of or serious injury to a child receiving a service, or the registration authority where a member of staff is referred for inclusion on the Protection of Children Act 1999 list held by the Secretary of State. Verbal notification must be confirmed in writing within 14 days.

Regulations 25–28 cover the requirements in relation to financial and managerial stability and action in the event of specified circumstances.

Regulation 29 makes it an offence to fail to comply with certain of the regulations.

Where more than one person is responsible for a required action, only one of them need do it to comply with the regulation [reg.30].

Regulations 31–33 amend the National Care Standards Commission (Registration) Regulations 2001, the National Care Standards Commission (Fees and Frequency of Inspections) (Adoption Agencies) Regulations 2003 and the Commission for Social Care Inspection (Fees and Frequency of Inspections) Regulations 2004 to include adoption support agencies.

Regulation 35 amends regulation 4 of the Adoption Information and Intermediary Services (Pre-Commencement Adoptions) Regulations 2005 to enable an adoption support agency to provide information to an adopted person from records it holds without being deemed to be providing an intermediary service.

The Special Guardianship Regulations 2005

These regulations apply in England only and relate to provision by local authorities of services to support special guardianship orders.

Local authorities are required to provide counselling, advice and information in relation to special guardianship (s.14F Children Act 1989) and the following prescribed services:

- financial support (see regulations 6–10);
- groups for children, their parents, special guardians and prospective special guardians;
- assistance, including mediation, with contact between children and their parents, relatives and others if beneficial to the child's welfare;
- therapeutic services for the child;
- support services including training, respite care and mediation [reg.3(1)].

Regulation 3(2) permits any of the prescribed services to include cash assistance.

Regulation 3(3) clarifies that any respite care accommodation must comply with ss.23 or 59 Children Act 1989.

Special guardianship support services may be provided by adoption agencies, adoption support agencies, health bodies and education authorities [reg.4].

Local authorities may provide special guardianship support services outside their area [reg.5(3)], and must do so for three years from the date of the order for:

Special Guardianship Regulations

- a child they are – or were immediately before the order – looking after;
- the special guardian or prospective special guardian of such a child;
- the children of such special guardians or prospective special guardians [reg.5(1) & (2)].

The cut-off period of three years does not apply to financial support agreed before the order was made [reg.5(2)].

Regulation 6 provides that financial support may be paid to:

- prospective special guardians to help them become a child's special guardian where this would benefit the child's welfare; or
- support special guardians in such cases after the order has been made [reg.6(1)].

Regulation 6(2) sets out the circumstances in which financial support may be paid:

- to enable a special guardian or prospective special guardian to look after a child;
- where a child needs greater expenditure on special care because of illness, disability, emotional or behavioural difficulty, or past abuse or neglect;
- to cover legal costs (including court fees) for a special guardianship application, a section 8 (Children Act 1989) application, or an order for financial provision for the child;
- to contribute to the child's accommodation and maintenance, including furniture and equipment, house alterations, transport, clothes, toys and other necessary items.

Financial support can only include a reward element if agreed in advance of the order where the special guardian or prospective special guardian was the child's foster carer and was receiving payments including a reward element for the child [reg.7(1)].

The reward element is payable for up to two years from the order unless the child has exceptional needs or there are exceptional circumstances [reg.7(2)].

Financial support may be paid periodically to meet recurring expenses (subject to the conditions in regulation 10(1)), in a lump sum, or in agreed instalments [reg.8].

Under regulation 9, financial support ends when the child:

- is no longer with the special guardian;
- finishes full-time education and starts work;
- qualifies for state benefits;
- reaches 18, unless continuing in full-time education, when it can continue until the course ends.

In order to receive periodic payments of financial support, the special guardian or prospective special guardian must agree to:

- notify the local authority immediately (and if orally, confirm in writing in seven days) of any new address, the child's death, any changes listed in regulation 9 and any change in financial circumstances or the financial needs or resources of the child;
- supply an annual statement of financial circumstances and the financial needs and resources of the child, plus confirmation of address and that the child is still there [reg.10(1)].

Local authorities may impose conditions on payments, including how and when they are to be spent [reg.10(2)].

Payments may be suspended or stopped if any conditions are not met, and the local authority may seek repayment of part or all of the amount paid; however, in the case of failure to supply an annual statement, the authority must first send a reminder giving 28 days to comply [reg.10(3) & (4)].

Local authorities must assess support needs at the request of a child who is (or was immediately before a special guardianship order) looked

Special Guardianship Regulations

after, a special guardian or prospective special guardian of such a child, or a parent of such a child [reg.11(1)].

Local authorities may assess support needs on receiving a written request from (or if a child, on behalf of):

- a child on a special guardianship order (or the subject of an application);
- a special guardian (or an applicant);
- a parent;
- a special guardian's child;
- anyone with a significant ongoing relationship with the child [reg.11(2)].

If minded not to assess where it has discretion, a local authority must advise the applicant with reasons, and give them a reasonable opportunity to make representations [reg.11(3)].

Assessments may be limited to a particular support service if it is specifically requested or seems the most appropriate provision [reg.11(4)].

Assessments must consider any of the following which are relevant:

- the child's development needs;
- the special guardian/prospective special guardian's parenting capacity;
- the child's family and background;
- the child's life with the special guardian/prospective special guardian;
- any previous assessments;
- the special guardian/prospective special guardian's needs and those of their family;

- the likely effect of a special guardianship order on relationships between the child, the parent and the special guardian/prospective special guardian [reg.12(1)].

The local authority must, if appropriate, interview the subject of any assessment, and if a child, also interview the special guardian/ prospective special guardian or any other appropriate adult [reg.12(2)].

If health or education services appear to be needed, the relevant body must be consulted as part of the assessment [reg.12(3)].

Local authorities must write a report of the assessment [reg.12(4)].

In deciding an amount of financial support, local authorities must take account of any grant, benefit, allowance or resource available to the person as a special guardian/prospective special guardian [reg.13(2)].

Unless regulation 13(4) or (5) applies, local authorities must also take account of:

- the person's financial resources, including state benefits payable for the child;
- the person's reasonable outgoings and commitments (excluding the child);
- the child's financial needs and resources [reg.13(3)].

Under regulation 13(4), local authorities must disregard the means test in regulation 13(3) if paying legal costs to support a special guardianship application for a looked after child.

Regulation 13(5) allows local authorities to disregard the regulation 13(3) means test when paying:

- setting up or special care costs for a child they looked after;
- ongoing travel costs for contact purposes;
- any reward element under regulation 7 [reg.13(5)].

Except for advice and information or one-off support, local authorities must draw up a support services plan [reg.14(2)].

Special Guardianship Regulations

If health or education services appear to be needed, the relevant body must be consulted before drawing up the plan [reg.14(3)].

Local authorities must nominate someone to monitor the plan's implementation [reg.14(4)].

People must be given the chance to make representations before a decision about support needs is made, having first been notified of the proposed decision and the time allowed for making representations [reg.15(1) & (2)].

The notice must state:

- the person's support needs;
- the basis for determining any financial support and the amount payable;
- if the local authority proposes to provide any support services, and if so which services;
- any conditions to be imposed [reg.15(3)].

If services are to be provided and a plan is required, a draft plan must accompany the notice [reg.15(4)].

No decision can be made until:

- the person has made representations or accepted the proposal and any draft plan; or
- the time limit has expired [reg.15(5)].

When the local authority has made a decision about providing support services, it must notify the person, with reasons [reg.16(1)].

If a plan is required, the notice must include the plan and the person nominated to monitor it [reg.16(2)].

For financial support, the notice must state:

- how the amount is calculated;

- the amount, frequency, period and start date of payments by instalments;
- the date of any one-off payment;
- any conditions attached, any date by which they are to be met and what happens if they are not met;
- review, variation and termination procedures;
- the local authority's and special guardian's or prospective special guardian's respective responsibilities with regard to reviews [reg.16(3)].

Reviews of periodic financial support are covered by regulation 18 and of other services by regulation 17.

Regulation 17(2) requires the local authority to review provision at least annually; and if the person's circumstances change; and at any other time appropriate to the plan.

Reviews must be conducted as for assessments in accordance with regulations 12 and 13 [reg.17(3)].

People must be given the chance to make representations before a decision about variation or termination of support services is made, having first been notified of the proposed decision and the time allowed for making representations. The notice must contain the information listed in regulation 15(3) and any revised draft plan [reg.17(4) & (5)].

Local authorities must make a decision about variation or termination based on the review and any representations, and if necessary revise the plan; they must then notify the person, with reasons and details of any revised plan [reg.17(6) & (7)].

Regulation 18(2) requires local authorities to review financial support on receipt of the annual statement, and if the person's circumstances change or any condition is breached, and at any other time appropriate to the plan.

Special Guardianship Regulations

Reviews must be conducted as for assessments in accordance with regulations 12 and 13 [reg.18(4)].

People must be given the chance to make representations before a decision to reduce or stop payments or revise the plan, having first been notified of the proposed decision and the time allowed for making representations. The notice must contain the information listed in regulation 15(3) and any revised draft plan [reg.18(5) & (7)].

Payments may be suspended pending a decision [reg.18(6)].

Local authorities must make a decision about variation, termination or recovery of any payments made, based on the review and any representations, and if necessary revise the plan; they must then notify the person, with reasons and details of any revised plan [reg.18(8) & (9)].

In urgent cases, the local authority may disregard any requirement to assess, plan or notify which would delay service provision [reg.19].

Regulation 20 requires notices to be in writing, and in the case of a child who is not of sufficient age or understanding or where the local authority deems it inappropriate, to be given to the special guardian or prospective special guardian or other appropriate adult.

Regulation 21 prescribes the content of court reports in special guardianship cases as set out in Schedule 1.

Regulation 22 clarifies that the local authority responsible under section 24 Children Act 1989 for a child subject to a special guardianship order is the one which last looked after the child.

PART III
NATIONAL MINIMUM STANDARDS

National Minimum Standards Adoption Agencies

These standards, **effective from 25.07.14**, are issued under sections 23 and 49 Care Standards Act 2000. They apply to adoption agencies and adoption support agencies (ASAs) in England, except as follows:

Standards 5, 13, 14 and 17 apply only to adoption agencies.

Standard 26 applies only to ASAs.

Standards 21, 23, 24 and 25 do not apply to ASAs if the registered provider is an individual without staff or volunteers, or is not required to appoint a registered manager.

Though not enforceable in themselves, they are used by the registration authority (Ofsted) in its regulatory role to determine whether agencies meet their obligations under the (mandatory) regulations, taking into consideration the additional contextual data of the adoption scorecards.

The standards are intended to be used by adoption agencies, ASAs and Ofsted to focus on securing positive outcomes for children, good quality services for service users, and reducing risks to their welfare and safety. They are an essential part of the overall responsibility to safeguard and promote the welfare of children and service users.

Note that the text of the Standards incudes reference to the Statutory Guidance on Adoption dated July 2014. This has not yet been issued and remains in draft form only. The 2013 Guidance is the only applicable Statutory Guidance at the time of writing.

CHILD & SERVICE USER FOCUSED STANDARDS

STANDARD 1 – The child's wishes and feelings

Underpinning legislation

Section 1 Adoption and Children Act 2002 (considerations applying to the exercise of powers)

Adoption Agencies Regulations 2005:

> Regulation 13 – Requirement to provide counselling and information for, and ascertain wishes and feelings of, the child
> Regulation 36 – Reviews
> Regulation 37 – Independent Reviewing Officers

Further guidance

Adoption and Children Act 2002 Statutory Guidance 2014 – Chapters 2 and 5

Outcome

Children know that their views, wishes and feelings are taken into account in all aspects of their care; are helped to understand why it may not be possible to act upon their wishes in all cases; and know how to obtain support and make a complaint.

Standard

1.1 Children's views, wishes and feelings are acted upon, unless this is contrary to their interests.

1.2 Children understand how their views have been taken into account and where significant wishes or concerns are not acted upon, they are helped to understand why.

1.3 No child is assumed unable to communicate their views and each child's preferred method of communication is known.

1.4 Children have access to independent advice and support from adults whom they can contact directly and in private about problems or concerns, which is appropriate to their age and understanding. Children know their rights to advocacy and how to access an advocate, and how to contact the Children's Rights Director.

1.5 Children can take up issues in the most appropriate way with support, without fear that this will result in any adverse consequences. Children receive prompt feedback on any concerns or complaints raised and are kept informed of progress (or lack of progress) throughout the adoption process, in a manner which is suitable to their age and understanding.

1.6 The wishes, feelings and views of children are taken into account by the adoption agency and adoption support agency in monitoring and developing its service.

STANDARD 2 – Promoting a positive identity, potential and valuing diversity

Underpinning legislation

Section 1 Adoption and Children Act 2002 (considerations applying to the exercise of powers)

Adoption Agencies Regulations 2005:

Regulation 13 – Requirement to provide counselling and information for, and ascertain wishes and feelings of, the child
Regulation 14 – Requirement to provide counselling and information for, and ascertain wishes and feelings of, the parent or guardian of the child and others
Regulation 15 – Requirement to obtain information about the child
Regulation 16 – Requirement to obtain information about the child's family
Regulation 17 – Requirement to prepare child's permanence report for the adoption panel
Regulation 24 – Requirement to provide preparation for adoption
Regulation 30 – Prospective adopter's report
Regulation 35 – Requirements imposed on the adoption agency before the child may be placed for adoption
Regulation 36 – Reviews

Adoption and Children Act 2002 Statutory Guidance 2014 – Chapters 1, 2 and 5

Outcome

Children have a positive self view, emotional resilience and knowledge and understanding of their background.

Standard

2.1   The adoption agency is active in its efforts to obtain for the child clear and appropriate information from the birth parents and birth families about:

   a. themselves and the child's birth and early life,
   b. why the child could not remain with their birth parents,
   c. why the child was placed for adoption,
   d. health issues of the birth parents and their children,
   e. the view of the birth parents and birth family about the adoption and contact, and
   f. up-to-date information about themselves and their situation.

2.2 The adoption agency is active in its efforts, after the adoption order is made, to encourage and support the birth parents and birth families to give the child, via the adoption agency, updates on significant family information.

2.3 Prospective adopters are prepared and supported to promote the child's social and emotional development, and to enable the child to develop emotional resilience and positive self-esteem.

2.4 Prospective adopters are helped and supported in understanding the importance of keeping safe any information provided by the birth family and in giving this information to their adopted child in an age-appropriate format when they feel the time is right, or on request when the young person reaches adulthood.

2.5 The preparation of the life story book is co-ordinated by one person, preferably the child's social worker.

2.6 The life story book represents a realistic and honest account of the circumstances surrounding the child's adoption. Its format is appropriate to the child's age and understanding and accessible for use by the child. Prospective adopters are encouraged to update it with the child as their understanding develops.

2.7 The life story book is given to the child and prospective adopters in stages: at the latest by the second statutory review of the child's placement with the prospective adopters; and the completed life story book at the latest within ten working days of the adoption ceremony.

2.8 The social worker who knows the child writes the later life letter. The letter is realistic and sufficiently detailed so that the young adult fully understands their life before adoption, why they could not remain with their birth parents, and why they were adopted. The prospective adopters receive the letter within ten working days of the adoption ceremony.

National Minimum Standards Adoption Agencies

STANDARD 3 – Promoting positive behaviour and relationships

Underpinning legislation

Adoption Agencies Regulations 2005:

> Regulation 15 – Requirement to obtain information about the child
> Regulation 17 – Requirement to prepare child's permanence report for the adoption panel
> Regulation 24 – Requirement to provide preparation for adoption
> Regulation 30 – Prospective adopter's report
> Regulation 36 – Reviews

Schedule 1 Information

Schedule 4 Information about the prospective adopter

Outcome

Children enjoy sound relationships with their prospective adopters, interact positively with others and behave appropriately.

Standard

3.1   Prospective adopters are prepared and supported to help the child develop positive relationships and behaviour and discourage negative behaviour, while assisting the child to understand and manage their own behaviour.

3.2   Prospective adopters are supported on how to manage their responses and feelings arising from caring for the child, particularly where the child displays very challenging behaviour, and understand how the child's previous experiences can manifest in challenging behaviour.

3.3 Prospective adopters are encouraged to respect the child's privacy and confidentiality, in a manner that is consistent with good parenting.

STANDARD 4 – Safeguarding children

Underpinning legislation

The Local Authority Adoption Service (England) Regulations 2003:

>Regulation 9 – Arrangements for the protection of children

The Voluntary Adoption Agencies and the Adoption Agencies (Miscellaneous Amendments) Regulations 2003:

>Regulation 10 – Arrangements for the protection of children

The Adoption Support Agencies (England) and Adoption Agencies (Miscellaneous Amendments) Regulations 2005:

>Regulation 12 – Arrangements for the protection of children

Adoption Agencies Regulations 2005:

>Regulation 24 – Requirement to provide counselling, information and preparation for adoption
>Regulation 25 – Requirement to carry out police checks
>Regulation 30 – Prospective Adopter's Report
>Regulation 36 – Reviews

Further guidance

Adoption and Children Act 2002 Statutory Guidance 2014 – Chapters 2 and 5

National Minimum Standards Adoption Agencies

Outcome

Children feel safe and are safe; children understand how to protect themselves and are protected from significant harm including neglect, abuse, and accident.

Standard

4.1   Children's safety and welfare are promoted and children are protected from abuse and other forms of significant harm (e.g. sexual or labour exploitation).

4.2   The adoption agency supports the prospective adopter to encourage the child to take appropriate risks as a normal part of growing up. Children are helped to understand how to keep themselves safe including when outside of the household or when using the internet or social media.

4.3   Adoption agencies and adoption support agencies work effectively with agencies concerned with child protection, e.g. the responsible authority, schools, hospitals, general practitioners, etc, and do not work in isolation from them.

STANDARD 5 – Promoting good health and wellbeing

Underpinning legislation

The Adoption Agencies Regulations 2005:

Regulation 15 – Requirement to obtain information about the child
Regulation 17 – Requirement to prepare child's permanence report for the adoption panel
Regulation 31 – Proposed placement

Regulation 35 – Requirements imposed on the adoption agency before the child may be placed for adoption
Regulation 36 – Reviews

Further guidance

Adoption and Children Act 2002 Statutory Guidance 2014– Chapters 1, 3 and 5

Outcome

Children live in a healthy environment where their physical, emotional and psychological health is promoted and where they are able to access the services they need to meet their health needs.

Standard

5.1 Children's physical and emotional and social development needs are promoted.

5.2 Children understand their health needs, how to maintain a healthy lifestyle and to make informed decisions about their own health.

5.3 Children are encouraged to participate in a range of positive activities that contribute to their physical and emotional health.

5.4 Children have prompt access to doctors and other health professionals, including specialist services (in conjunction with the responsible authority), when they need these services.

5.5 Children's health is promoted in accordance with the child's permanence report, and prospective adopters are clear about what responsibilities and decisions are delegated to them and where consent for medical treatment needs to be obtained.

5.6 Children's wishes and feelings are sought and taken into account in their health care, according to their understanding, and prospective adopters advocate on behalf of children.

STANDARD 6 – Leisure activities

Underpinning legislation

Adoption Agencies Regulations 2005:

> Regulation 15 – Requirement to obtain information about the child
> Regulation 17 – Requirement to prepare child's permanence report for the adoption panel
> Regulation 24 – Requirement to provide preparation for adoption
> Regulation 31 – Proposed placement
> Regulation 36 – Reviews

Schedule 1 – Information

Further guidance

Adoption and Children Act 2002 Statutory Guidance 2014 – Chapters 1, 3 and 5

Outcome

Children are able to enjoy their interests, develop confidence in their skills and are supported and encouraged to engage in leisure activities.

Standard

6.1 Children develop their emotional, intellectual, social, creative and physical skills through the accessible and stimulating environment created within the prospective adopters' home. Children are supported to take part in school-based and out of school activities.

6.2 Children pursue individual interests and hobbies. They take part in a range of activities, including leisure activities and trips.

STANDARD 7 – Promoting educational attainment

Underpinning legislation

Adoption Agencies Regulations 2005:

Regulation 15 – Requirement to obtain information about the child
Regulation 17 – Requirement to prepare child's permanence report for the adoption panel
Regulation 24 – Requirement to provide preparation for adoption
Regulation 31 – Proposed placement
Regulation 35 – Requirements imposed on the adoption agency before the child may be placed for adoption
Regulation 36 – Reviews

Further guidance

Adoption and Children Act 2002 Statutory Guidance 2014 – Chapters 1, 3 and 5

Outcome

The education and achievement of children is actively promoted as valuable in itself and as part of their preparation for adulthood. Children are supported to achieve their educational potential.

Standard

7.1   Children have access to a range of educational resources to support their learning and have opportunities beyond the school day to engage in activities which promote learning.

7.2   Children are supported to attend school or alternative provision regularly.

7.3 Children are helped by their prospective adopters to achieve their educational or training goals and prospective adopters are supported to work with the child's education provider to maximise each child's achievements and to minimise any underachievement.

7.4 The placing agency has, and is fully implementing, a written education policy that promotes and values children's education.

7.5 Prospective adopters maintain regular contact with the child's school and other education settings, attending all parents' meetings as appropriate and advocating for the child where appropriate.

7.6 Prospective adopters engage and work with schools, colleges and other organisations, to support the child's education including advocating to help overcome any problems the child may be experiencing in their education setting.

STANDARD 8 – Contact

Underpinning legislation

Sections 1, 26, 27 & 46 Adoption and Children Act 2002

Section 8 Children Act 1989

Adoption Agencies Regulations 2005:

Regulation 13 – Requirement to provide counselling and information for, and ascertain wishes and feelings of, the child
Regulation 14 – Requirement to provide counselling and information for, and ascertain wishes and feelings of, the parent or guardian of the child and others
Regulation 15 – Requirement to obtain information about the child

National Minimum Standards Adoption Agencies

Regulation 17 – Requirement to prepare child's permanence report for the adoption panel

Regulation 18 – Function of the adoption panel in relation to a child referred by the adoption agency

Regulation 24 – Requirement to provide preparation for adoption

Regulation 31 – Proposed placement

Regulation 32 – Function of adoption panel in relation to proposed placement

Regulation 35 – Requirements imposed on the adoption agency before the child may be placed for adoption

Regulation 36 – Reviews

Regulations 46 and 47 – Contact

Adoption Support Services Regulations 2005:

Regulation 3 – Prescribed services

Regulation 4 – Persons to whom adoption support services must be extended

Further guidance

Adoption and Children Act 2002 Guidance 2014 – Chapters 1–3, 5–7

Statutory guidance Court orders and pre-proceedings April 2014

Outcome

Contact with birth parents, siblings, other members of the birth family and significant others is arranged and maintained when it is beneficial to the child.

Standard

8.1 Initial contact arrangements are focused on the child's needs with the views of the prospective adopters and birth family members taken into account. The arrangements are reviewed in accordance with the adoption support plan.

8.2 Where siblings cannot be placed together with the same prospective adopters or adopters, contact arrangements with other siblings are made when it is in the best interests of each of the children.

8.3 Prospective adopters are helped through training and support to understand the importance for the child of contact with birth parents, siblings, members of the birth family and significant others.

8.4 The adoption agency helps individuals comply with the agreed contact arrangements through practical support, and helps manage any difficult emotional or other issues they may have because of contact. In so doing, the agency takes full account of the child's age and level of understanding, and the individual capacities of all other parties.

8.5 Children, prospective adopters, adopters, birth parents and members of the birth family are helped to understand the harm unauthorised or unmediated contact, including through online social networks, can have and are supported if unauthorised contact is made. Prospective adopters are prepared in case this happens and are supported if it does happen.

STANDARD 9 – Providing a suitable physical environment for the child

Underpinning legislation

Adoption Agencies Regulations 2005:

Regulation 24 – Requirement to provide counselling, information and preparation for adoption
Regulation 30 – Prospective adopter's report
Regulation 31 – Proposed placement
Regulation 36 – Reviews

Further guidance

Adoption and Children Act 2002 Statutory Guidance 2014 – Chapters 3 and 5

Outcome

Children live with prospective adopters whose home provides adequate space, to a suitable standard. The child enjoys access to a range of activities which promote their development.

Standard

9.1 The adoption agency ensures during the assessment of the prospective adopters' suitability to adopt, that the prospective adopters' home can comfortably accommodate all who live there. It is warm, adequately furnished and decorated, free of avoidable hazards, is maintained to a good standard of cleanliness and hygiene and is in good order throughout. Outdoor spaces that are part of the premises are safe, secure and well maintained.

9.2 The adoption agency has a written policy concerning safety for children in the prospective adopters' home, and in vehicles used to transport the child, which is regularly reviewed in line with the most recent guidance from relevant bodies. The policy is understood and successfully implemented by prospective adopters.

STANDARD 10 – Recruiting and assessing prospective adopters

Underpinning legislation

Adoption Agencies Regulations 2005:

Regulation 21 – Registration of interest in adoption
Regulation 22 – Prospective adopter stage one plan
Regulation 24 – Requirement to provide counselling, information and preparation for adoption
Regulation 25 – Requirement to carry out police checks
Regulation 27 – Pre-assessment decision
Regulation 29 – Prospective adopter assessment plan
Regulation 30 – Prospective adopter's report
Regulation 30B – Adoption agency decision and notification

Restrictions on the Preparation of Adoption Reports Regulations 2005

Suitability of Adopters Regulations 2005

Further guidance

Adoption and Children Act 2002 Statutory Adoption Guidance 2014 – Chapter 3

Outcome

The adoption agency approves prospective adopters who can meet most of the needs of looked after children who are to be placed for adoption and who can provide them with a home where the child will be able to recover from the impact of their early life experience of loss and trauma, feel loved, safe and secure.

Standard

10.1 The adoption agency implements an effective strategy to recruit and assess prospective adopters who can meet most of the needs of those children for whom adoption is the plan. The agency monitors and evaluates the success of the strategy.

10.2 People who are interested in becoming adoptive parents, and prospective adopters, are treated fairly, without prejudice, openly and with respect. They are kept informed, on a regular basis, of the progress (or lack of progress) of their enquiry/application throughout the adoption process, in a manner which meets their individual communication needs. They are given regular opportunities to raise any specific concerns or questions, which are then answered as directly and fully as possible.

10.3 The assessment process is clearly explained to adopters, including:
   a. eligibility criteria;
   b. preparation, assessment and approval procedure, including checks and references, timescales and the prospective adopters' right to make representation to the adoption agency or apply to the Secretary of State for an independent review if the adoption agency considers them unsuitable to adopt at Stage Two of the process;
   c. children who need adoptive families both locally and the wider national profile. For VAAs, examples of the range of children awaiting adoption;
   d. matching, introduction and placement process, including the Adoption and Children Act Register;
   e. eligibility and entitlement to adoption support services;
   f. the adoption agency's expectations of prospective adopters.

10.4 Agencies respond to requests for detailed information (following initial enquiries either to the National Gateway for Adoption or directly to an adoption agency) within ten working days, through an information session, a visit, a planned telephone call or a similar arrangement with the prospective adopter.

10.5 The adoption agency issues registration of interest form to the prospective adopters when they consider the prospective adopters are ready to begin Stage One of the process. On receipt of the form, the agency decides within five working days whether to accept this. Where agencies are not currently recruiting, or do not currently have the capacity, they refer the prospective adopter to the National Gateway for Adoption or another agency which they know is recruiting.

10.6 The agency completes Stage One of the adopter approval process within two months and Stage Two within four months unless there is good reason for not doing so or on request of the prospective adopter. The agency allows the prospective adopter to take an active role, advised by the agency, in the Stage One process. Certain previous adopters or approved foster carers are allowed to enter at Stage Two and receive a tailored assessment agreed by the agency and the applicants.

10.7 Applicants are given the opportunity to talk to approved adopters, adoptees and birth parents whose children were adopted.

10.8 Preparation courses are held and made available to all prospective adopters, including foster carers who wish to adopt the child for whom they are caring. Preparation courses fit within a framework of equal opportunities and anti-discriminatory practice and are organised to encourage and facilitate attendance by prospective adopters, for example, by including convenient times and venues. The effectiveness of preparation received is evaluated and reviewed annually.

10.9 Prospective adopters are prepared to become adoptive parents in a sensitive way, which addresses and gives them skills, knowledge and practical techniques to manage the issues they are likely to encounter, and identifies the competencies and strengths they have or will need to develop. Preparation courses should give encouragement to prospective adopters, showing them the positive aspects of parenting a child as well as helping them to understand, for example:
   a. the difficulties some children experience, such as the traumas of neglect and abuse, and the effect on their development and capacity to form secure attachments;
   b. the key parenting skills and parenting capacities they need to care for children who have experienced neglect and abuse;
   c. an understanding of the significance of the child's identity, their birth family, the need for openness to help the child to reflect on and understand their history, according to their age and ability; the role of contact, how to manage

unauthorised contact, including through online social networks; and the importance of significant memorabilia.

10.10 Prospective adopters understand why status and health checks, personal references and enquiries are undertaken about them and enhanced police checks are required/made on themselves and adult members of their household.

10.11 Prospective adopters are considered in terms of their capacity to look after children in a safe and responsible way that meets the child's development needs.

10.12 The adoption team manager checks that the prospective adopter's report is accurate, up-to-date and has evidence-based information which distinguishes between fact, opinion and third party information, before it is submitted to the adoption panel. The social worker who wrote the prospective adopter's report signs and dates it. The report is countersigned and dated by the adoption team manager (or a team manager of another adoption team within the agency) and the prospective adopters.

STANDARD 11 – Intercountry – assessing prospective adopters

Underpinning legislation

Adoptions with a Foreign Elements Regulations 2005:

Regulation 13 – Requirements applicable in respect of eligibility and suitability
Regulation 14 – Counselling and information
Regulation 15 – Procedure in respect of carrying out an assessment

Restrictions on the Preparation of Adoption Reports Regulations 2005:

Suitability of Adopters Regulations 2005

National Minimum Standards Adoption Agencies

Further guidance

Adoption and Children Act 2002 Statutory Adoption Guidance 2014 – Chapter 3

Outcome

The adoption agency approves prospective adopters who can meet most of the needs of children who live outside the British Islands and who can provide them with a home where the child will be able to recover from the impact of their early life experience of loss and trauma, feel loved, safe and secure.

Standard

11.1 People who are interested in becoming adoptive parents, and prospective adopters, are treated fairly, without prejudice, openly and with respect. They are kept informed, on a regular basis, of the progress (or lack of progress) of their enquiry/application throughout the adoption process, in a manner which meets their individual communication needs. They are given regular opportunities to raise any specific concerns or questions, which are then answered as directly and fully as possible.

11.2 The assessment process is clearly explained to prospective adopters, including:

a. the intercountry adoption process;
b. details of requirements imposed upon prospective adopters by English legislation;
c. information about the country or countries they wish to adopt from, including the eligibility criteria;
d. any laws governing adoption which the chosen country has in place that they must operate within;
e. details of fees involved in the application and post approval process;
f. preparation, assessment and approval procedure, including checks, references, timescales and the prospective adopter's right to make representation to the adoption agency or apply

to the Secretary of State for an independent review if the adoption agency considers them unsuitable to adopt at Stage Two of the approval process;

g. adoption support;
h. the adoption agency's expectation of prospective adopters; and
i. how the adoption agency prioritises applications to adopt children from outside the British Islands and looked after children, including how they are referred on to other adoption agencies.

11.3   Agencies respond to requests for detailed information (following initial enquiries either to the National Gateway for Adoption or directly to an adoption agency) within ten working days, through an information session, a visit, a planned telephone call or a similar arrangement with the prospective adopter.

11.4   The adoption agency issues registration of interest form to the prospective adopters when they consider the prospective adopters are ready to begin Stage One of the process. On receipt of the form the agency decides within five working days whether to accept this. Where agencies are not currently recruiting, or do not currently have the capacity, they refer the prospective adopter to the National Gateway for Adoption or another agency which they know is recruiting.

11.5   The agency completes Stage One of the adopter approval process within two months and Stage Two within four months unless there is good reason for not doing so or on request of the prospective adopter. The agency allows the prospective adopter to take an active role, advised by the agency, in the Stage One process. Certain previous adopters or approved foster carers are allowed to enter at Stage Two and receive a tailored assessment agreed by the agency and the applicants.

11.6   Applicants are given the opportunity to talk to approved adopters and adoptees.

11.7 Preparation courses are held and made available to all prospective adopters, including foster carers who wish to adopt the child for whom they are caring. Preparation courses fit within a framework of equal opportunities and anti-discriminatory practice and are organised to encourage and facilitate attendance by prospective adopters, for example, by including convenient times and venues. The effectiveness of preparation received is evaluated and reviewed annually.

11.8 Prospective adopters are prepared to become adoptive parents in a sensitive way, which addresses and gives them skills, knowledge and practical techniques to manage the issues they are likely to encounter, and identifies the competencies and strengths they have or will need to develop. Preparation courses should give encouragement to prospective adopters, showing them the positive aspects of parenting a child as well as helping them to understand, for example:
- the impact of institutional care;
- the difficulties some children experience, such as the traumas of neglect and abuse, and the effect on their development and capacity to form secure attachments;
- the key parenting skills and parenting capacities they need to care for children who have experienced neglect and abuse and who may be of a different ethnic or cultural background to the applicants;
- an understanding of the significance of the child's identity, their birth family, the need for openness to help the child to reflect on and understand their history, according to their age and ability; the role of contact, how to manage unauthorised contact, including through online social networks; and the importance of significant memorabilia.

11.9 Prospective adopters understand why status and health checks, personal references and enquiries are undertaken about them and enhanced criminal records checks are required/made on themselves and adult members of their household.

11.10 Prospective adopters are considered in terms of their capacity to look after children in a safe and responsible way that meets the child's development needs.

11.11 The adoption team manager checks that the prospective adopter's report is accurate, up-to-date and has evidence-based information which distinguishes between fact, opinion and third party information, before it is submitted to the adoption panel. The social worker who wrote the prospective adopter's report signs and dates it. The report is countersigned and dated by the adoption team manager (or a team manager of another adoption team within the agency) and the prospective adopters.

STANDARD 12 – Birth parents and birth families involved in the adoption plan

Underpinning legislation

Adoption Agencies Regulations 2005:

> Regulation 14 – Requirement to provide counselling and information for, and ascertain wishes and feelings of, the parent or guardian of the child and others
> Regulation 15 – Requirement to obtain information about the child
> Regulation 16 – Requirement to obtain information about the child's family

Adoptions with a Foreign Element Regulations 2005:

> Regulation 37 – Counselling and information for the parent or guardian of the child etc

Further guidance

Adoption and Children Act 2002 Statutory Guidance 2014– Chapter 2

National Minimum Standards Adoption Agencies

Outcome

Children have clear and appropriate information about themselves, their birth parents and families and life before their adoption.

Birth parents and birth families take an active part in the planning and implementation of their child's adoption.

Standard

12.1 Birth parents and birth families are treated fairly, without prejudice, openly and with respect. They are kept informed, on a regular basis, of the progress (or lack of progress) of their child's adoption. They are given regular opportunities to raise any specific concerns or questions, which are then answered as directly and fully as possible.

12.2 A pregnant woman and the unborn baby's father, who are considering relinquishing their unborn baby for adoption, receive pre-birth counselling and from that understand the permanence options for their baby's future; how an adoption order would affect their unborn baby, themselves and their family; and are able to make an informed decision about the future of their unborn child.

12.3 Birth parents are given access to, and are actively encouraged to use, a support worker from the time adoption is identified as the plan for the child. The support worker is independent of the child's social worker.

12.4 Birth parents are given information on how to obtain legal advice, contact details of local and national support groups and services, and support to fulfil agreed plans for contact.

12.5 The wishes and feelings of the birth parents, siblings and other members of the birth family, and other people the agency considers relevant, are listened to and are valued and respected. They are taken into account when making decisions. Where they are not acted upon, the reasons for not doing so are explained to the individual so that they understand why their views are not reflected in their child's care. The wishes and feelings and, if applicable, the reasons why they are not being acted upon, are recorded on the child's case record and included in the child's permanence report.

12.6 Birth parents are helped to work through their concerns through the counselling they receive and understand what is proposed for their child and how the child will benefit if they take an active part in their child's adoption.

12.7 Birth parents are given the opportunity to comment on what is written about them or their circumstances before the information is passed to the adoption panel or to the child's proposed adoptive parents.

12.8 The adoption agency is active in its efforts to involve the birth parents and birth family in the adoption plan.

12.9 The adoption agency ensures the prospective adopters understand the importance for the birth family to be told if their child dies during childhood or soon afterwards and agrees to notify the adoption agency. The prospective adopters' decision and any subsequent action are recorded on their case record.

STANDARD 13 – Matching and placing the child with prospective adopters who can meet most of their assessed needs

Underpinning legislation

Section 1 Adoption and Children Act 2002 (Considerations applying to the exercise of powers)

Section 18 – Placement for adoption by agencies

Section 19 – Placing children with parental consent

Section 21 – Placement orders

Section 22 – Applications for placement orders

Adoption Agencies Regulations 2005:

Regulation 19 – Adoption agency decision and notification
Regulation 19A – Referral to the Adoption and Children Act Register – children
Regulation 30G – Referral to the Adoption and Children Act Register – prospective adopters
Regulation 31 – Proposed placement
Regulation 35 – Requirements imposed on the adoption agency before the child may be placed for adoption

Further guidance

Adoption and Children Act 2002 Statutory Adoption Guidance 2014 – Chapters 4 and 5

Outcome

Children benefit from stable placements and are matched and placed with prospective adopters who can meet most, if not all, of their assessed needs.

Children feel loved, safe and secure with their prospective adoptive parents with whom they were originally placed; and these children were placed within the timeframe set out in the adoption scorecard indicators A1 (average time between a child entering care and moving in with his or her adoptive family, for children who have been adopted) and A2 (average time between a local authority receiving court authority to place a child and the local authority deciding on a match with an adoptive family)[1].

---

1   The scorecard indicators are in Annex B of the Statutory Guidance and on www.gov.uk

National Minimum Standards Adoption Agencies

Standard

13.1 The child's details are referred to the Adoption and Children Act Register when no locally identified match is being actively pursued at the latest by three months after the agency's decision-maker has decided that the child should be placed for adoption.

13.2 The prospective adopter's details are referred to the Adoption Register as soon as they have been approved as suitable to adopt if they consent and it seems unlikely that there will be a placement with a child in their area, or at three months when no locally identified match is being actively pursued. Prospective adopters are advised that they may refer themselves to the Adoption Register three months after their approval.

13.3 The consent of the birth parents to their child being placed for adoption is sought, or an application for a placement order is made as part of the care proceedings, immediately after the decision of the agency's decision-maker that the child should be placed for adoption, bearing in mind that any delay is likely to prejudice the child's welfare.

13.4 The Prospective Adopter's Report and the Child's Permanence Report are used to identify prospective adopters who can meet the majority, if not all, of the child's needs as set out in the Child's Permanence Report.

13.5 When a match is being considered, the placing agency will provide the prospective adopter's social worker access to the whole content of the child's adoption case record so that they may be fully aware of the child's background, health, emotional and developmental needs and practical implications for parenting that child.

13.6 The agency has met with the prospective adopters and has discussed with them the proposed placement and the implications for them and their family; ascertained the views of the prospective adopters and, as far as possible, provided them with a counselling service and access to specialist medical/educational advice.

13.7 The prospective adopters are helped to fully understand the child's background, health, emotional and developmental needs and the practical implications for parenting that child before they agree for the match to be passed to the adoption panel.

13.8 The adoption agency has procedures for introducing a child to the prospective adopters and others living in the household that can be adapted to the individual needs of the child and prospective adopters.

13.9 The prospective adopters are invited to attend the placement planning meeting and are given a copy of the placement plan.

13.10 The child and prospective adopters feel well prepared before the placement and are happy with the pace of the introductions and the date of placement. The child visits the prospective adopters' home before the date the child moves into the home.

13.11 The child is given information about the prospective adopters, their home and, when applicable, their children, family and pets before they are placed with prospective adopters. The child knows whether they will have their own bedroom, which school they will be attending, and is given information about the local area, facilities and activities.

13.12 The child knows how they may contact their social worker and understands the contact arrangements with birth parents, members of their birth family, and significant others.

STANDARD 14 – Intercountry – matching prospective adopters to child's assessed needs

Underpinning legislation

Adoptions with a Foreign Element Regulations 2005:

> Regulation 19 – Procedure following receipt of the Article 16 Information from the Central Authority of the State of origin

Outcome

Children feel loved, safe and secure with their adoptive parents or prospective adoptive parents.

Standard

14.1 The agency has met with the prospective adopters and has discussed with them the proposed placement and the implications for them and their family; ascertained the views of the prospective adopters and, as far as possible, provided them with a counselling service and access to specialist medical/ educational advice.

14.2 The prospective adopters are helped to fully understand the child's background, health, emotional and developmental needs and the practical implications for parenting that child before they accept the match.

14.3 The prospective adopters are helped to understand the importance of keeping safe any information provided by the birth family, adoption agency or body in the child's State of origin and gives this information to their adopted child on request, or when they feel the time is right.

National Minimum Standards Adoption Agencies

14.4 The prospective adopters are helped to understand the importance for the birth family to be told if their child dies during childhood or soon afterwards and agrees to notify the adoption agency. The prospective adopters' decision and any subsequent action are recorded on their case record.

14.5 The prospective adopters understand the importance of commissioning post placement/post adoption reports consistent with any undertakings prospective adopters have given to the State of origin.

STANDARD 15 – Adoption support

Underpinning legislation

The Adoption Support Services Regulations 2005

The Local Authority Adoption Service (England) Regulations 2003:

> Regulation 9A – Provision of services

The Voluntary Adoption Agencies and the Adoption Agencies (Miscellaneous Amendments) Regulations 2003:

> Regulation 24F – Provision of services

The Adoption Support Agencies (England) and Adoption Agencies (Miscellaneous Amendments) Regulations 2005:

> Regulation 13 – Provision of services

Further guidance

Adoption and Children Act 2002 Statutory Guidance 2014 – Chapter 9

Outcome

Children and adults affected by adoption receive an assessment of their adoption support needs.

Service users confirm that the adoption support services provided met or are meeting their assessed needs.

Standard

15.1 Where services are commissioned by an adoption agency, a three-way working relationship is developed with the adoption agency and the adoption support agency working in partnership to most effectively meet the needs of the service user. Commissioning arrangements are underpinned by a written agreement and are reviewed at regular intervals.

15.2 When deciding whether to provide a service, or which service to provide, the agency has regard to the assessed needs for adoption support services, listens to the service user's wishes and feelings, and considers their welfare and safety.

15.3 The service user knows, and receives written information about, the service they are to receive; what the service is designed to achieve; what is involved in the particular service provision; and how the service will be monitored to ensure that it is delivering the intended outcome.

15.4 Prospective adopters and adopters are made aware of, and encouraged by, the Adoption Support Services Adviser to access support services, and apply for tax credits and welfare benefits which are available to them and advise them of their employment rights to leave and pay.

15.5 The Adoption Support Services Adviser assists prospective adopters and adopters through liaison with education and health services, across local authority boundaries and between departments within the local authority.

15.6 Adoption agencies seek feedback from service users on the success of the service provision. This feedback is recorded centrally and on the case record of the service user.

STANDARD 16 – Intermediary services

Underpinning legislation

Sections 9 and 98 Adoption and Children Act 2002

Adoption Information and Intermediary Services (Pre-commencement Adoptions) Regulations 2005

Further guidance

Adoption and Children Act 2002 Statutory Guidance 2014 – Chapter 10

Practice Guidance on Adoption – Access to Information and Intermediary Services

Outcome

Adopted adults and birth relatives are assisted to obtain information in relation to the adoption, where appropriate, and contact is facilitated between an adopted adult and their birth relative if that is what both parties want.

Standard

16.1 Information is provided about the Adoption Contact Register and how to register a wish for contact or no contact, and about absolute and qualified vetoes and the potential benefits and disadvantages of registering a veto.

16.2 The applicant is met and their identity verified before any information is disclosed to them, contact facilitated, or a veto is registered.

16.3 The appropriate adoption agency and the intermediary agency agree a timescale for responding to an enquiry and keeps the intermediary agency informed of the progress (or lack of progress) of their enquiry.

16.4 Service users are helped to understand the possible effects on them and their family of the outcome of their search.

16.5 Service users are consulted on decisions made in relation to their service provision. Consultation with service users is recorded on their individual records.

16.6 Agencies seek feedback from service users on the success of the service provision. This feedback is recorded centrally and on the case record of the service user.

THE ADOPTION AGENCY/ADOPTION SUPPORT AGENCY STANDARDS

STANDARD 17 – Adoption panels and agency's decision-maker

Underpinning legislation

Section 1 Adoption and Children Act 2002 Considerations applying to the exercise of powers

Adoption Agencies Regulations 2005:

Part 2 – Adoption Agency (regulations 3–8)

> Regulation 18 – Function of the adoption panel in relation to a child referred by the adoption agency

National Minimum Standards Adoption Agencies

Regulations 19 and 30B – Adoption agency decision and notification
Regulation 30A – Function of the adoption panel
Regulation 32 – Function of the adoption panel in relation to proposed placement
Regulation 33 – Adoption agency decision in relation to proposed placement

Further guidance

Adoption and Children Act 2002 Statutory Guidance 2014 – Chapters 1–3 and 8

Outcome

The adoption panel and decision-maker make timely, quality and appropriate recommendations/decisions in line with the overriding objective to promote the welfare of children throughout their lives.

Standard

17.1 The adoption agency implements clear written policies and procedures on the recruitment to and maintenance of the central list of persons considered by them to be suitable to be members of an adoption panel ('the central list') and constitution of the adoption panel.

17.2 Adoption panels provide a quality assurance feedback to the agency every six months on the quality of reports being presented to the panel. This includes whether the requirements of the Restrictions on the Preparation of Adoption Reports Regulations 2005 have been met, and whether there is a thorough, rigorous, consistent and fair approach across the service in the assessment of whether a child should be placed for adoption, the suitability of prospective adopters and the proposed placement. This sub-standard is linked to standard 25.

17.3 Adoption panels meet at least one day every month to consider cases before it unless it is an adoption panel of a small voluntary adoption agency[2] when it meets at least every six weeks to consider the suitability of a prospective adopter to adopt a looked after child or the termination of approval of a prospective adopter.

17.4 All necessary information is provided to panel members at least five working days in advance of the panel meeting to enable full and proper consideration.

17.5 Prospective adopters are given the opportunity to attend and be heard at all adoption panel meetings which discuss their brief or full prospective adopter's report prepared on their suitability to adopt a child, or termination of their approval, as applicable.

17.6 Adoption panels make a considered recommendation on whether the child should be placed for adoption within six weeks of the statutory review where adoption was identified as the permanence plan.

17.7 The adoption panel makes a considered recommendation on the proposed placement of a child with particular prospective adopters within six months of the adoption agency's decision-maker deciding that the child should be placed for adoption.

17.8 Where these timescales have not been met, the panel records the reasons in the written minutes of the panel meeting.

17.9 The panel Chair ensures written minutes of panel meetings are accurate and clearly cover the key issues and views expressed by panel members and record the reasons for its recommendation.

17.10 The decision-maker makes a considered decision that takes account of all the information available to them, including the recommendation of the adoption panel and, where applicable, the independent review panel, within seven working days of receipt of the recommendation and final set of panel minutes.

---

2 Seven full-time social workers or the equivalent but not including the manager or branch manager as defined in the Chief Inspector of Education, Children's Services and Skills (Fees and Frequency of Inspection) (Children's Homes) Regulations 2007

National Minimum Standards Adoption Agencies

17.11 The child's birth parents and prospective adopters, as appropriate, are informed orally of the decision-maker's decision within two working days and written confirmation is sent to them within five working days.

STANDARD 18 – Statement of Purpose and Children's Guides

Underpinning legislation

The Local Authority Adoption Service (England) Regulations 2003:

Regulation 2 – Statement of purpose
Regulation 3 – Children's guide
Regulation 4 – Review of statement of purpose and children's guide

Schedules 1 and 2

The Voluntary Adoption Agencies and the Adoption Agencies (Miscellaneous Amendments) Regulations 2003:

Regulations 3 and 24B – Statement of purpose
Regulation 4 – Review of statement of purpose
Regulation 24C – Children's guide

The Adoption Support Agencies (England) and Adoption Agencies (Miscellaneous Amendments) Regulations 2005:

Regulation 5 – Statement of purpose and children's guide
Regulation 6 – Review of statement of purpose and children's guide

National Minimum Standards Adoption Agencies

Outcome

Children, service users and staff are clear about the aims and objectives of the adoption agency/adoption support agency, and what services and facilities it provides.

The adoption agency/adoption support agency meets the aims and objectives in the Statement of Purpose.

Standard

18.1   The adoption agency and adoption support agency has a clear statement of purpose which is available to and understood by staff, volunteers, children, birth parents and guardians, prospective adopters and adopters, and is reflected in any policies, procedures and guidance.

18.2   The aims and objectives of the statement of purpose should be outcome focused and, for adoption agencies, show how the service will meet outcomes for children.

18.3   The adoption agency (in the case of a local authority, the executive side of that local authority; in the case of a VAA, the registered provider and manager)/registered person of the adoption support agency formally approves the statement of purpose and children's guides, and reviews them at least annually.

18.4   The agency's policies, procedures and any written guidance to staff and volunteers accurately reflect the statement of purpose.

Children's guide to adoption

18.5   The local authority gives the child a copy of the children's guide to adoption after the decision-maker has decided that the child should be placed for adoption and after being counselled as required by reg.13 of the Adoption Agencies Regulations 2005. The guide is appropriate to the child's age and understanding and includes a summary of what happens at each stage (including at court) and how long each stage is likely to take. The

National Minimum Standards Adoption Agencies

children's guide also contains information on how a child can find out their rights, how they can contact their Independent Reviewing Officer (IRO), the Children's Rights Director, Ofsted, if they wish to raise a concern with inspectors, and how to secure access to an independent advocate.

Children's guide to adoption support

18.6 The children's guide to adoption support services is provided to the child by the adoption agency or adoption support agency which is providing adoption support. The guide is appropriate to the child's age and understanding and includes a summary of what the service sets out to do for children and is given to all children and/or their representatives. The children's guide also contains information on how a child can find out their rights, how they can contact their Independent Reviewing Officer, the Children's Rights Director, Ofsted, if they wish to raise a concern with inspectors, and how to secure access to an independent advocate.

STANDARD 19 – Fitness to provide or manage an adoption agency or an adoption support agency

Standard 19.2(c) and (f), 19.3(d) and (f) and 19.4–19.6 do not apply in respect of adoption support agencies where the registered provider is an individual and does not have staff or volunteers.

Underpinning legislation

The Local Authority Adoption Service (England) Regulations 2003:

Regulation 5 – Appointment of manager
Regulation 6 – Fitness of manager

The Voluntary Adoption Agencies and the Adoption Agencies (Miscellaneous Amendments) Regulations 2003:

> Regulation 5 – Fitness of registered provider
> Regulation 6 – Appointment of manager and branch manager
> Regulation 7 – Fitness of manager and branch manager

The Adoption Support Agencies (England) and Adoption Agencies (Miscellaneous Amendments) Regulations 2005:

> Regulation 7 – Fitness of registered provider
> Regulation 8 – Appointment of manager
> Regulation 9 – Fitness of manager
> Regulation 10 – Registered person – general requirements

Outcome

The agency is provided and managed by those who are suitable to work with children and have the appropriate skills, experience and qualifications to deliver an efficient and effective service.

Standard

19.1 The people involved in carrying on and managing the adoption agency or adoption support agency:

   a. have the knowledge and experience of adoption law and practice, and when providing services to children, knowledge and experience of child care law and practice;
   b. have business and management skills to manage the work efficiently and effectively; and
   c. have financial expertise to ensure that the agency is run on a sound financial basis and in a professional manner.

Adoption agency manager and branch manager

19.2 The manager and branch manager has on taking up the post:

a. a recognised social work qualification or a professional qualification, at least at Level 4,[3] relevant to working with children; and
b. at least two years' experience relevant to adoption within the past five years; and
c. at least one year's experience supervising and managing professional staff; and
d. in-depth knowledge and experience of child care law and practice; and
e. where the agency provides an intercountry adoption service, knowledge of:
    i. intercountry legislation and practice;
    ii. the principles of the law and eligibility criteria for the overseas country;
    iii. the Hague Convention on Protection of Children and Cooperation in respect of Intercountry Adoption;
    iv. the immigration rules and immigration legislation that apply to the country in question; and
    v. the implications for children who are (a) adopted from outside the British Islands and (b) being taken out of the British Islands for the purposes of adoption; and
f. the adoption agency manager has a qualification in management at least at Level 4.

Registered manager of an adoption support agency

19.3 The registered manager (or registered provider, where the registered provider is an individual and there is no registered manager) of an adoption support agency has on taking up the post:

---

3 With respect to standard 19.2 (a) and (f), 19.3 (a) and (d) and 19.4, for persons undertaking a qualification after January 2011, the relevant qualification will be the Level 5 Diploma in Leadership for Health and Social Care and Children and Young People's Services. Managers who already hold a Level 4 Leadership and Management for Care Services and Health and Social Care will not need to undertake this qualification at Level 5.

a. a recognised social work qualification, or a professional qualification, at least at Level 4, relevant to working in an adoption setting (or children's services where the agency provides services to children); or

b. is a Member (MBACP) or Accredited Member (MBACP Accred) of the British Association of Counselling and Psychotherapy (BACP), or is chartered by/registered with the United Kingdom Council for Psychotherapy (UKCP), or the United Kingdom Register for Counsellors and Psychotherapists (UKRCP); or

c. is registered as an Arts, Drama or Music Therapist or as a Practitioner Psychologist with the Health Professions Council for England and Wales (HPC); and

d. a qualification in management at least at Level 4; and

e. at least two years' experience relevant to adoption within the past five years; and

f. at least one year's experience of supervising and managing professional staff.

All managers of adoption agencies and adoption support agencies (or registered provider of an adoption support agency where the registered provider is an individual and there is no registered manager)

19.4 Appointees to the post of manager who have no management qualifications must enrol on a management training course within six months, and obtain a relevant management qualification within three years of appointment.

19.5 The responsibilities and duties of the manager and to whom they are accountable are clear and understood by them. The manager is notified in writing of any change in the person to whom they are accountable.

19.6 The manager exercises effective leadership of the staff and operation, such that the agency is organised, managed and staffed in a manner that delivers the best possible child care (in respect of adoption agencies)/service provision for the agency's service users (in respect of adoption agencies/adoption support agencies).

STANDARD 20 – Financial viability and changes affecting business continuity

Underpinning legislation

The Voluntary Adoption Agencies and the Adoption Agencies (Miscellaneous Amendments) Regulations 2003:

> Regulation 20 – Financial position

The Adoption Support Agencies (England) and Adoption Agencies (Miscellaneous Amendments) Regulations 2005:

> Regulation 25 – Financial position

Outcome

The voluntary adoption agency/adoption support agency is financially sound.

Standard

20.1 A qualified accountant certifies that the annual accounts indicate the service is financially viable and likely to have sufficient funding to continue to fulfil its statement of purpose for the next 12 months.

20.2 The adoption agency/adoption support agency has a written development plan, reviewed annually, for the future of the agency, either identifying any planned changes in the operation or resources of the agency, or confirming the continuation of the agency's current operation and resourcing.

20.3 Where the agency, for any reason, cannot adequately and consistently maintain its services which comply with regulations or NMS, an effective plan must be established and implemented either to rectify the situation or to close down the service.

STANDARD 21 – Suitability to work with children and service users

This standard is not relevant in respect of adoption support agencies where the registered provider is an individual and does not have staff or volunteers.

Underpinning legislation

The Local Authority Adoption Service (England) Regulations 2003:

Regulation 10 – Staffing agency
Regulation 11 – Fitness of workers
Regulation 12 – Employment of staff

The Voluntary Adoption Agencies and the Adoption Agencies (Miscellaneous Amendments) Regulations 2003:

Regulation 11 – Staffing of agency
Regulation 14 – Fitness of workers
Regulation 15 – Employment of staff

The Adoption Support Agencies (England) and Adoption Agencies (Miscellaneous Amendments) Regulations 2005:

Regulation 18 – Staffing of agency
Regulation 19 – Fitness of workers
Regulation 20 – Employment of staff

National Minimum Standards Adoption Agencies

Outcome

There is careful selection of all staff, volunteers and persons on the central list and there is monitoring of such people to help prevent unsuitable people from having the opportunity to harm children and service users.

Standard

21.1 All people working in or for the purposes of the agency, and persons applying to be included on the central list, are interviewed as part of the selection process and have references checked to assess suitability before taking up their duties. Telephone enquiries are made to each referee to verify the written references.

21.2 The agency can demonstrate, including from written records, that it consistently follows good recruitment practice, and all applicable current statutory requirements and guidance in the recruitment of staff, volunteers and persons on the central list. This includes Disclosure and Barring Service (DBS) checks. All personnel responsible for recruitment and selection of staff are trained in, understand and operate these good practices.

21.3 The agency has a record of the recruitment and suitability checks which have been carried out for staff, volunteers and persons on the central list which includes:

   a. identity checks;
   b. DBS disclosures, including the level of the disclosure and the unique reference number (in line with eligibility to obtain such checks);
   c. checks to confirm qualifications which are a requirement and others which are considered by the agency to be relevant;
   d. at least two references, preferably one from a current employer, and where possible, a statement from each referee as to their opinion of the person's suitability to work with children;
   e. checks to confirm the right to work in the UK;

f. where the person has lived outside of the UK, further checks as are considered appropriate where obtaining a DBS disclosure is not sufficient to establish suitability to work with children.

21.4 The record must show the date on which each check was completed and should show who carried out the check. The DBS disclosure information must be kept in secure conditions and must be destroyed by secure means as soon as it is no longer needed in line with the DBS Code of Practice. Before the disclosure is destroyed, records need to be kept as described above.

21.5 The agency's system for recruiting staff and others includes an effective system for reaching decisions as to who is to be appointed and the circumstances in which an application should be refused in relation to staff or others, in the light of any criminal convictions or other concerns about suitability that are declared or discovered through the recruitment process.

21.6 There is a whistle-blowing policy which is made known to all staff, volunteers and persons on the central list. This makes it a clear duty for such people to report to an appropriate authority any circumstances within the agency which they consider likely to significantly harm the safety, rights or welfare of any child placed by the service.

STANDARD 22 – Handling allegations and suspicions of harm

Underpinning legislation:

The Local Authority Adoption Service (England) Regulations 2003:

Regulation 9 – Arrangements for the protection of children

The Voluntary Adoption Agencies and the Adoption Agencies (Miscellaneous Amendments) Regulations 2003:

> Regulation 10 – Arrangements for the protection of children
> Regulation 19 – Notifiable events

The Adoption Support Agencies (England) and Adoption Agencies (Miscellaneous Amendments) Regulations 2005:

> Regulation 12 – Arrangements for the protection of children
> Regulation 24 – Notifiable events

Outcome

Allegations and suspicions of harm are handled in a way that provides effective protection and support for children, the person making the allegation, and at the same time supports the person who is the subject of the allegation.

Standard

22.1 All adoption agency and adoption support agency staff and volunteers understand what they must do if they receive an allegation or have suspicions that a person may have:

   a. behaved in a way that has, or may have, harmed a child;
   b. possibly committed a criminal offence against or related to a child; or
   c. behaved towards a child in a way that indicates they are unsuitable to work with children.

   The agency ensures that the required actions are taken, or have been taken, in any relevant situation of which it is aware.

22.2 The agency's procedure is in line with Government guidance and requirements, including the duty to refer information to statutory bodies. It is known to staff, volunteers, prospective adopters and children.

22.3 A copy of the child protection procedures is made available to staff, volunteers, prospective adopters and children. Any

National Minimum Standards Adoption Agencies

comments on these procedures are taken into account by the agency.

22.4 The child protection procedures are submitted for consideration and comment to the Local Safeguarding Children Board (LSCB) and to the Local Authority Designated Officer (LADO) for Child Protection (or other senior officer responsible for child protection matters in that department). They are consistent with the local policies and procedures agreed by the LSCB relevant to the geographical area where the prospective adopters live. Any conflicts between locally agreed procedures and those of other placing authorities are discussed and resolved as far as possible.

22.5 Each agency has a designated person, who is a senior manager, responsible for managing allegations. The designated person has responsibility for liaising with the LADO and for keeping the subject of the allegation informed of progress during and after the investigation.

22.6 Allegations against people that work with children, prospective adopters or adult members of their household, are reported by the agency to the LADO. This includes allegations that on the face of it may appear relatively insignificant or that have also been reported directly to the police or Children and Family Services.

22.7 A clear and comprehensive summary of any allegations made against a prospective adopter or member of the prospective adopters' household, or staff member or volunteer, including details of how the allegation was followed up and resolved, a record of any action taken and the decisions reached, is kept on the prospective adopter's or person's confidential file. A copy is provided to the person as soon as the investigation is concluded. The information is retained on the confidential file, even after someone leaves the organisation, until the person reaches normal retirement age or for ten years if this is longer. In respect of prospective adopters or adult members of their household, the information is retained on their case record for 100 years from the date of the adoption order or, if the prospective adopter does not adopt a child, for a period of time according to local policies.

22.8 The adoption panel that dealt with the case is informed of any allegations made and outcomes of investigations.

22.9 Investigations into allegations or suspicions of harm are handled fairly, quickly, and consistently in a way that provides effective protection for the child, and at the same time supports the person who is the subject of the allegation. Agencies follow the framework for managing cases of allegations of abuse against people who work with children as set out in Working Together to Safeguard Children.

22.10 There is written guidance for staff which makes clear how they will be supported.

22.11 During an investigation the agency makes support, which is independent of the agency, available to the person subject to the allegation.

22.12 The adoption support agency has written procedures for dealing with allegations of historical abuse which may be made by service users during the course of service provision.

STANDARD 23 – Learning, development and qualifications

This standard is not relevant in respect of adoption support agencies where the registered provider is an individual and does not have staff or volunteers.

Underpinning legislation

The Local Authority Adoption Service (England) Regulations 2003:

Regulation 12 – Employment of staff

The Voluntary Adoption Agencies and the Adoption Agencies (Miscellaneous Amendments) Regulations 2003:

Regulation 15 – Employment of staff

The Adoption Support Agencies (England) and Adoption Agencies (Miscellaneous Amendments) Regulations 2005:

Regulation 20 – Employment of staff

The Adoption Agencies Regulations 2005:

Regulation 3 – The central list

Outcome

Children and service users receive a service from staff, volunteers, panel members and decision-makers who have the competence to meet their needs.

Standard

23.1 There is a good quality learning and development programme, which includes induction, post-qualifying and in-service training, that staff and volunteers are supported to undertake. The programme equips them with the skills required to meet the needs of the children and service users, keeps them up-to-date with professional, legal and practice developments and reflects the policies, legal obligations and business of the agency.

23.2 The learning and development programme is evaluated for effectiveness at least annually and if necessary is updated.

23.3 All new staff undertake the Children's Workforce Development Council's induction standards, commencing within seven working days of starting their employment and completing them within six months (this requirement does not apply to ASAs where the agency works only with adults).

23.4 Where the agency provides an intercountry adoption service, training is provided to staff, volunteers and persons on the central list:

   a. on intercountry legislation and practice;
   b. on the principles of the law and eligibility criteria for the overseas country;
   c. on the Hague Convention on Protection of Children and Cooperation in respect of Intercountry Adoption;
   d. on the immigration rules and immigration legislation that apply to the country in question;
   e. and the implications for children who are (a) adopted from outside the British Islands and (b) being taken out of the British Islands for the purposes of adoption.

23.5 Assessment and appraisal of all staff involved in adoption takes account of identified skills needed for particular roles and is used to identify individuals' learning and development needs.

Qualifications

23.6 All social workers and other specialists (e.g. medical, legal, educationalists, psychologists, therapists) are professionally qualified and, where applicable, registered by the appropriate professional body. They are appropriately trained to work with children, their families and adoptive families, and have a good understanding of adoption.

23.7 All counsellors are either a Member (MBACP) or Accredited Member (MBACP Accred) of the British Association of Counselling and Psychotherapy; or are chartered by/registered with the United Kingdom Council for Psychotherapy (UKCP), or the United Kingdom Register for Counsellors and Psychotherapists (UKRCP).

23.8 All arts, drama and music therapists and practitioner psychologists are registered with the Health Professions Council for England and Wales. Other staff who are involved in the provision of therapeutic services have appropriate professional qualifications.

Birth records counselling and disclosure of adoption information

23.9 Social workers providing birth records counselling under Schedule 2 to the ACA 2002 and social workers and counsellors providing disclosure of adoption information counselling[4] are trained and experienced in this kind of counselling and have a thorough understanding of the legislation surrounding access to, and disclosure of, birth records, and the impact of reunion on all parties.

23.10 Any individual who provides disclosure of adoption information counselling who is not a social worker or counsellor, works under the direct supervision of a social worker or counsellor experienced in that work and who takes responsibility for the counselling.

Other staff

23.11 Where unqualified staff and volunteers carry out social work functions, they do so under the direct supervision of experienced social workers, who are accountable for their work.

23.12 Support workers working with birth parents have a good knowledge and understanding of adoption legislation and process and work under the direct supervision of experienced social workers, who are accountable for their work.

Persons on the central list

23.13 The adoption agency provides each person on the central list with an opportunity of observing an adoption panel meeting before they sit on an adoption panel.

---

4 Disclosure of adoption information counselling to adults under the Adoption Information and Intermediary Services (Pre-commencement Adoptions) Regulations 2005 and the Disclosure of Adoption Information (Post-commencement Adoptions) Regulations 2005 – see Part II of this guide.

23.14 Each person on the central list is given induction training which is completed within 10 weeks of being included on the central list.

23.15 Each person on the central list is given the opportunity of attending an annual joint training day with the agency's adoption staff.

23.16 Each person on the central list has access to appropriate training and skills development and is kept abreast of relevant changes to legislation, regulation and guidance.

Adoption agency's decision-maker

23.17 The decision-maker is a senior person within the adoption agency or is a trustee or director of the voluntary adoption agency, who is a social worker with at least three years' post-qualifying experience in child care social work and has knowledge and experience of permanency planning for children; adoption and child care law and practice; and where the adoption agency provides an intercountry adoption service, knowledge of:

   i. intercountry legislation and practice;
   ii. the principles of the law and eligibility criteria for the overseas country;
   iii. the Hague Convention on Protection of Children and Cooperation in respect of Intercountry Adoption;
   iv. the immigration rules and immigration legislation that apply to the country in question; and
   v. the implications for children who are (a) adopted from outside the British Islands and (b) being taken out of the British Islands for the purposes of adoption and when determining the disclosure of protected information about adults (s.61 Adoption and Children Act 2002), understands the legislation surrounding access to and disclosure of information, and the impact of reunion on all parties.

STANDARD 24 – Staff support and supervision

This standard is not relevant in respect of adoption support agencies where the registered provider is an individual and does not have staff or volunteers.

Underpinning legislation

The Local Authority Adoption Service (England) Regulations 2003:

> Regulation 10 – Staffing agency
> Regulation 12 – Employment of staff

The Voluntary Adoption Agencies and the Adoption Agencies (Miscellaneous Amendments) Regulations 2003:

> Regulation 11 – Staffing of agency
> Regulation 15 – Employment of staff

The Adoption Support Agencies (England) and Adoption Agencies (Miscellaneous Amendments) Regulations 2005:

> Regulation 18 – Staffing of agency
> Regulation 20 – Employment of staff

Outcome

Staff and volunteers are supported and guided to fulfil their roles and provide a high quality service to children and service users.

Standard

24.1 The employer is fair and competent, with sound employment practices and good support for all its staff and volunteers.

24.2 All staff, volunteers and manager, are properly managed, supported and understand to whom they are accountable.

National Minimum Standards Adoption Agencies

24.3 Suitable arrangements exist for professional supervision of managers and the registered person of the agency.

24.4 Staff have access to support and advice, and are provided with regular supervision by appropriately qualified and experienced staff.

24.5 A written record is kept by the agency detailing the time and date and length of each supervision held for each member of staff, including the registered person. The record is signed by the supervisor and the member of staff at the end of the supervision.

24.6 All staff have their performance individually and formally appraised at least annually and, where they are working with children, this appraisal takes into account the views of the children the service is providing for.

24.7 Staff and volunteers are able to access the specialist advice needed to provide a comprehensive service for children and service users, including medical, legal, educationalists', psychologists' and therapists' advice.

STANDARD 25 – Managing effectively and efficiently, and monitoring the adoption agency or adoption support agency

This standard is not relevant in respect of adoption support agencies where the registered provider is an individual who is not required to appoint a registered manager.[5]

5 If the registered provider is an individual, they are only required to appoint a manager if they are (a) not a fit person to manage the agency or (b) not, or not intending to be, in full-time day-to-day charge of the agency. See Regulation 9 of the Adoption Support Agencies (England) and Adoption Agencies (Miscellaneous Amendments) Regulations 2005.

Underpinning legislation

The Local Authority Adoption Service (England) Regulations 2003:

    Regulation 7 – General requirements
    Regulation 14 – Arrangements for absence of manager
    Regulation 17 – Complaints

The Voluntary Adoption Agencies and the Adoption Agencies (Miscellaneous Amendments) Regulations 2003:

    Regulation 8 – Registered provider, manager and branch manager – general requirements
    Regulations 11 and 12 – Complaints
    Regulation 21 – Notice of absence

The Adoption Support Agencies (England) and Adoption Agencies Regulations 2005:

    Regulation 10 – Registered person – general requirements
    Regulations 16 and 17 – Complaints
    Regulation 26 – Notice of absence

Outcome

The agency is managed ethically, effectively and efficiently and delivering a good quality service which meets the needs of children and other service users.

Standard

25.1   There are clear and effective procedures for monitoring and controlling the activities of the agency. This includes the financial viability of the service, any serious incidents, or allegations, or complaints about the service and ensuring quality of the agency.

25.2   The manager regularly monitors all records kept by the agency to ensure compliance with the agency's policies, to identify any concerns about specific incidents and to identify patterns and trends. Immediate action is taken to address any issues raised by this monitoring.

25.3 Management of the agency ensures all staff's work and activity is consistent with adoption regulations and NMS and with the service's policies and procedures.

25.4 Managers, staff and volunteers are clear about their roles and responsibilities. The level of delegation and responsibility of the manager and the lines of accountability, are clearly defined.

25.5 Clear arrangements are in place to identify the person in charge when the manager is absent.

25.6 The executive side of the local authority, the voluntary adoption agency's/adoption support agency's provider/trustees, board members or management committee members:

   a. receive written reports on the management, outcomes and financial state of the agency every six months;
   b. monitor the management and outcomes of the services in order to satisfy themselves that the agency is effective and is achieving good outcomes for children and/or service users;
   c. satisfy themselves that the agency is complying with the conditions of registration.

25.7 The agency takes action to address any issues of concern that they identify or which is raised with them.

25.8 Staff and volunteers have a copy of:

   a. the policies and working practices in respect of grievances and disciplinary matters;
   b. the details of the services offered;
   c. the equal opportunities policy;
   d. the health and safety procedures.

25.9 Information is provided to commissioners of services as part of tendering. This includes:

   a. charges for each of its services;
   b. statements of any amounts paid to adopters; and

National Minimum Standards Adoption Agencies

    c. amounts paid for services, e.g. health and education.

25.10 The agency has written policy and procedural guidelines on considering and responding to representations and complaints in accordance with legal requirements and relevant statutory guidance.

25.11 The agency has the facilities to work with children, potential service users and service users with physical, sensory and learning impairment, communication difficulties, or for whom English is not their first language.

25.12 Oral and written communications are made available in a format which is appropriate to the physical, sensory and learning impairments, communication difficulties, and language of the individual. The procedures include arrangements for reading, translating, Makaton, pictures, tape recording and explaining documents to those people who are unable to understand the document.

STANDARD 26 – Individuals who are registered providers of adoption support agencies

This standard is relevant only where the registered provider is an individual (as opposed to a partnership or organisation) and they do not have staff or volunteers.

Underpinning legislation

The Adoption Support Agencies (England) and Adoption Agencies (Miscellaneous Amendments) Regulations 2005:

    Regulation 10 Registered person – general requirements
    Regulations 16 and 17 – Complaints

Outcome

The registered provider manages the agency effectively and efficiently and is suitable to work with the agency's service users. They are trained to ensure the best possible outcomes for service users.

Standard

26.1 The registered provider has regular supervision with appropriately qualified and experienced persons.

26.2 A written record is kept detailing the time and date and length of each supervision. The record is signed by the supervisor and the registered provider at the end of the supervision.

26.3 The registered provider undertakes ongoing training and appropriate professional and skills development and keeps up-to-date with current issues in the adoption field and developments in legislation and guidance.

26.4 The registered provider monitors the management and outcome of the services in order to be satisfied that the agency is effective and is achieving good outcomes for children and/or service users and that the agency is complying with the conditions of registration.

26.5 Information is provided to commissioners of services as part of tendering. This includes charges for each of its services and itemised amounts paid for services.

26.6 The registered provider has written policy and procedural guidelines on considering and responding to representations and complaints in accordance with legal requirements and relevant Government guidance.

26.7 The registered provider has the facilities to work with children, potential service users and service users with physical, sensory and learning impairments, communication difficulties or for whom English is not their first language.

National Minimum Standards Adoption Agencies

26.8 Oral and written communications are made available in a format which is appropriate to the physical, sensory and learning impairments, communication difficulties, and language of children, potential service users, service users, staff, volunteers and persons on the central list. The procedures include arrangements for reading, translating, Makaton, pictures, tape recording and explaining documents to those people who are unable to understand the document.

26.9 The registered provider has a comprehensive written health and safety policy and equal opportunities policy for all service users which covers all legal requirements.

STANDARD 27 – Records

Underpinning legislation

The Adoption Agencies Regulations 2005:

Regulation 12 – Requirement to open the child's case record
Regulation 23 – Prospective adopter's case record

The Local Authority Adoption Service (England) Regulations 2003:

Regulation 15 – Records with respect to staff

The Voluntary Adoption Agencies and the Adoption Agencies (Miscellaneous Amendments) Regulations 2003:

Regulation 17 – Records with respect to staff

Disclosure of Adoption Information (Post-Commencement Adoptions) Regulations 2005

The Adoption Support Agencies (England) and Adoption Agencies (Miscellaneous Amendments) Regulations 2005:

Regulation 14 – Records with respect to services

National Minimum Standards Adoption Agencies

Regulation 15 – Adoption case records (adoption support agencies that were formerly adoption agencies)
Regulation 22 – Records with respect to staff

Outcome

Records are clear, accurate, up to date and stored securely, and contribute to an understanding of the child's life.

Standard

27.1   The agency has and implements a written policy that clarifies the purpose, format and content of information to be kept on the agency's files, on the child's and prospective adopters' case records.

27.2   Staff, volunteers and persons on the central list understand and follow the agency's policy for the keeping and retention of files, managing confidential information and access to files (including files removed from the premises). There is a system in place to monitor the quality and adequacy of record keeping and take action when needed.

27.3   Staff understand and follow the agency's[6] policy on dealing with requests for access to or disclosure from adoption case records and know who is responsible for authorising them. They obtain a written confidentiality agreement from the person to whom the agency wishes to disclose the case records or information. This requirement does not cover the child or adopter.

27.4   Entries in records, decisions and reasons are legible, clearly expressed, non-stigmatising, distinguish between fact, opinion and third party information and are signed and dated.

---

6   This standard applies to all adoption agencies. It applies also to those ASAs who were a VAA prior to 30.12.05 and whose registration was changed to that of an ASA with effect from 30.12.05, and for whom reg.16(2A) of the Adoption Agencies Regulations 1983 permitted them to retain their pre-30 December 2005 adoption records on children and prospective/approved adopters.

27.5 There is a system for keeping records of all complaints made and for handling these confidentially and securely. Records of complaints and allegations are clearly recorded on the relevant files for staff, volunteers, children and service users – including details of the investigation, conclusion reached and action taken. Separate records are also kept which bring together data on allegations and on complaints.

STANDARD 28 – Fitness of premises for use as an adoption agency or adoption support agency

Underpinning legislation

The Voluntary Adoption Agencies and the Adoption Agencies (Miscellaneous Amendments) Regulations 2003:

> Regulation 18 – Fitness of premises

The Local Authority Adoption Service (England) Regulations 2003:

> Regulation 16 – Fitness of premises

The Adoption Support Agencies (England) and Adoption Agencies (Miscellaneous Amendments) Regulations 2005:

> Regulation 23 – Fitness of premises

Outcome

The premises and administrative systems are suitable to enable the agency to meet its Statement of Purpose.

National Minimum Standards Adoption Agencies

Standard

28.1 There are efficient and robust administrative systems, including IT and communication systems. Premises have:

 a. facilities for the secure retention of records (including, for example, cards, letters; the child's life story book; photographs and audiovisual film).
 b. appropriate measures to safeguard IT systems; and
 c. an appropriate security system.

28.2 The premises and its contents are insured (or there are alternative prompt methods of replacing lost items).

28.3 The agency has a business continuity plan, which staff understand and can access, which includes both provision of premises and safeguarding/back-up of records.

STANDARD 29 – Notification of significant events

Underpinning legislation

The Voluntary Adoption Agencies and the Adoption Agencies (Miscellaneous Amendments) Regulations 2003:

 Regulation 19 – Notifiable events

The Adoption Support Agencies (England) and Adoption Agencies (Miscellaneous Amendments) Regulations 2005:

 Regulation 24 – Notifiable events

Outcome

All significant events relating to the protection of children are notified to the appropriate authorities.

Standard

29.1 The registered provider and the manager of the VAA/registered person of the adoption support agency has a system in place to notify, within 24 hours, persons and appropriate authorities of the occurrence of significant events in accordance with regulation 19 or regulation 24. The system includes what to do where a notifiable event arises at the weekend.

29.2 A written record is kept which includes details of the action taken, and the outcome of any action or investigation, following a notifiable event.

29.3 The registered provider and the manager of the VAA/registered person of the adoption support agency has a system for notification to responsible authorities of any serious concerns about the emotional or mental health of a child, such that a mental health assessment would be requested under the Mental Health Act 1983.

29.4 Following an incident notifiable under regulation 19 or regulation 24, the registered provider and the manager of the VAA/registered person of the adoption support agency contacts the responsible authority to discuss any further action that may need to be taken.

Appendix 1: Source material

Primary legislation

Adoption and Children Act 2002
Children Act 1989
Children and Young Persons Act 2008
Children and Families Act 2014
Education and Adoption Act 2016
Children and Social Work Act 2017

Subordinate legislation

The Adoption Agencies Regulations 2005
The Adoption Support Services Regulations 2005
The Independent Review of Determinations (Adoption and Fostering) Regulations 2009
The Adoptions with a Foreign Element Regulations 2005
The Adopted Children and Adoption Contact Registers Regulations 2005
The Adoption Information and Intermediary Services (Pre-Commencement Adoptions) Regulations 2005
The Disclosure of Adoption Information (Post-Commencement Adoptions) Regulations 2005
The Restriction on the Preparation of Adoption Reports Regulations 2005
The Suitability of Adopters Regulations 2005
Adoption Support Agencies (England) and Adoption Agencies (Miscellaneous Amendments) Regulations 2005
The Special Guardianship Regulations 2005
DfE Statutory Adoption Guidance July 2013
The Care Planning, Placement and Case Review Regulations 2010
The Care Planning, Placement and Case Review and Fostering Services (Miscellaneous Amendments) Regulations 2013
The Adoption Agencies (Panel & Consequential Amendments) Regulations 2012

Appendix 1: Source material

The Adoption Agencies (Miscellaneous Amendments) Regulations 2013

National Minimum Standards

Adoption National Minimum Standards 2014

Index

A
Access to agency records 45
Adoption
    Advance consent 18
    Annulment 59
    Baby 17, 99
    By one person or couple 43
    Contact register 54, 127
    Overseas 58
    Panel 81
    With a foreign element 55
Adoption service 8
Adoption society 8
Adoption support 9, 104
Adoption support agency 12, 154
Advertisements 75
Advocacy 155
Agency records 103, 133, 207, 210
Appeals 62
Applications
    Adoption 43
    Contact 22
    Placement order 19
Appropriate adoption agency 128
Assessments 10
Authority to place 15

B
Baby adoption 17, 99
Brief report 93

C
CAFCASS 64

Central authority 122
Central list 81
Civil partner 19, 43
Contact register 54, 127
Child arrangements order 68
Children and young people's plans 12
Child's case record 84
Child's permanence report 86
Conditions of making an adoption order 40
Consent
    Adoption 40, 42
    Placement 16, 18, 26
    Withdrawal 19, 102
Contact
    Agency responsibility 22, 100, 161
    Section 8 orders 24
    Section 26 orders 22
    Section 34 orders 23
Counselling 49, 84, 107, 132, 176, 202

D

Delay – avoidance 5, 66
Determinations 115
Disclosure
    Consent 132
    Counselling 49, 132
    Court documents 133
    Information 45, 133
    Information to adopted adult 47, 135
    Offence 47, 133
    Protected information 45, 135
Domicile 42

E

Evidence of consent 66

F

Fast track assessment 95

Fees 55, 82, 129, 133
Foreign element 58, 117
Foster carers 33, 34, 68, 147
Fostering for Adoption 17, 80, 103

G
Guardian 17, 27, 43

H
Habitual residence 43
Hague Convention 59, 121
Household 88

I
Independent Review 12, 94, 115
Inspection of premises 13
Intercountry adopters 97
Intermediary service 129

J
Joint panel 82

K

L
Local authority foster carers 33, 34, 68, 147

M
Matching 97
Meaning of adoption 50
Medical adviser 81, 85
Minimum standards
    Adoption agency 155

N
Name 28, 117
National minimum standards – see minimum standards
Non-agency adoption 37
Notice of intention to adopt 37

O

Offences 47, 58, 77, 129, 133, 138
Overseas adoption 61, 117

P

Paramountcy 5
Parental consent 17, 43
Parental responsibility 22, 56
Partners of parents 34
Permanence Report, Child's 86
Placement 15, 21, 24, 43, 98
Placement order
    Applications 19
    Pre-conditions 18
    Revoking 21
    Varying 21
Placement plan 101
Pre-conditions for adoption 35, 40
Preliminaries to adoption 36
Prohibitions 62
Prospective adopters 15, 36
Protected information 45, 133, 134, 164

Q

Qualifying determinations 115

R

Recovery
    Child placed 30
    Child not placed 29
Regional adoption agencies 10
Register
    Adopted children 52, 127
    Adoption contact 54, 127
Relative
    Adoptive 51
Reports

Adoption placement 98, 139
　　　Child's permanence 85, 134
　　　Prospective adopter's 92, 138
Restrictions on taking child out of UK 57
Reviews
　　　Approved adopters 96
　　　Children 101
Revocation of placement orders 21

S
Status of adopted child 50
Suitability to adopt 35, 38, 88, 90, 92, 96, 97, 138
Serving of notice 66
Special guardianship 66, 144

T
Training 89, 106, 203, 204

U
Unmarried couple 43

V
Variation
　　　Contact order 24
　　　　　Placement order 21
Veto 131

W
Welfare checklist 5
Witnessing consent 18, 66, 88

XYZ